Beginner's URDU script

Richard Delacy

TEACH YOURSELF BOOKS

For UK order queries: please contact Bookpoint Ltd, 78 Milton Park, Abingdon, Oxon OX14 4TD. Telephone: (44) 01235 400414, Fax: (44) 01235 400454. Lines are open from 9.00–6.00, Monday to Saturday, with a 24 hour message answering service.
Email address: orders@bookpoint.co.uk

For U.S.A. & Canada order queries: please contact NTC/Contemporary Publishing, 4255 West Touhy Avenue, Lincolnwood, Illinois 60646–1975, U.S.A.
Telephone: (847) 679 5500, Fax: (847) 679 2494.

Long renowned as the authoritative source for self-guided learning – with more than 30 million copies sold worldwide – the *Teach Yourself* series includes over 200 titles in the fields of languages, crafts, hobbies, business and education.

British Library Cataloguing in Publication Data
A catalogue record for this title is available from The British Library.

Library of Congress Catalog Card Number: On file

First published in UK 2001 by Hodder Headline Plc, 338 Euston Road, London, NW1 3BH.

First published in US 2001 by NTC/Contemporary Publishing, 4255 West Touhy Avenue, Lincolnwood (Chicago), Illinois 60646–1975 U.S.A.

Typeset by ASK Language Services Ltd.
Printed in Great Britain for Hodder & Stoughton Educational, a division of Hodder Headline Plc, 338 Euston Road, London NW1 3BH by Cox & Wyman Ltd, Reading, Berkshire.

Impression number	10 9 8 7 6 5 4 3 2 1
Year	2006 2005 2004 2003 2002 2001

CONTENTS

INTRODUCTION

The Urdu script

The Urdu language is written is a modified form of the Persian script which is in turn a modified form of the Arabic script. This modification takes the form of the addition of characters to represent sounds that occur in Urdu but are not found in Arabic or Persian. In addition to Urdu, Persian and Arabic, the same script is used to write several other languages in India, Pakistan and Afghanistan, including Kashmiri, Punjabi and Pashto. There are two styles of this script: **nasta‘līq** and **naskh**. The basic difference between these styles is minor. Whereas in **naskh** words tend to run along the bottom line, in the more cursive **nasta‘līq** style they tend to slant diagonally from the top line to the bottom line.

السّلام علیکم	السّلام علیکم
nasta‘līq	**naskh**

While the **naskh** style of writing lends itself to type printing, texts written in the **nasta‘līq** style are still mostly prepared by a calligrapher and then printed using a technique called lithography. Both **naskh** and **nasta‘līq** fonts have been developed for use in computer software programs. The **nasta‘līq** style is conventionally employed in most Urdu texts, although the **naskh** style, which is used to write both Arabic and Persian, is occasionally used in some scholarly publications and reference books. Because of the continued predominance of **nasta‘līq** to write Urdu, it is this style with which the student will have to become most familiar and which is, therefore, treated in this book.

The Urdu script runs from right to left except for numerals, which are written from left to right. The alphabet contains thirty-five characters, each of which possesses a name. For example, the first character in the alphabet is called **alif** and is used to represent several vowel sounds in Urdu.

ا
alif

The script is cursive, in that the characters are joined together to form words. There are no capital letters. Most characters are made up of a basic linear portion and one, two, or three dots or another symbol that resembles a 'flat' symbol in music. These are written either above or below the linear portion of the character. The basic shape of some of the characters is the same and, for this reason, the alphabet is traditionally arranged in series of characters that have a similar basic form but are differentiated by the number or position of accompanying dots etc. For example, the second series of the alphabet comprises five characters, all of which have the same shape but a different number of dots or the symbol that resembles a flat sign in music.

ث 5	ٹ 4	ت 3	پ 2	ب 1
se	**ṭe**	**te**	**pe**	**be**

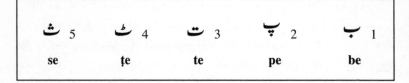

While all characters join to the preceding character in a word, not all join to the character that follows. Therefore, characters are conventionally considered to be of two types: those that join to characters on both sides and those that join only to the preceding character. Characters that join on both sides are called **connectors** while those that join only to the preceding character are called **non-connectors**. The shape of connecting characters also varies more or less depending on whether they occur at the beginning, in the middle or at the end of a word. There is also an independent form of characters, which occurs at the end of a word following a non-connector. It is the independent form that appears in the alphabet. Characters that do not connect to the following character have essentially only two forms, an initial and a final form. The initial form is the same as the independent form because it does not join to the following character and the final form is the same as the medial form for the same reason.

Another important feature of this script is that there are no characters to represent the three short vowels in Urdu. This makes learning how to pronounce new words difficult. There are, however, three symbols that may be employed to indicate which of these short vowels is present. There is also a symbol that is used to indicate when no vowel is pronounced with a character. These four symbols are rarely provided by writers because Urdu readers simply know the pronunciation of many of the words they read. However, they are always included in the Holy Quran to guarantee accurate pronunciation as well as in children's primers and dictionaries. They have also been used throughout this book with new words wherever they appear. Other features of the Urdu script include both the existence of several characters that represent more or less the same sound for Urdu speakers and also characters that may represent more than one sound. For example, there are four characters that represent the sound **z** and two characters that may each represent three vowels and a semi-vowel. There also exist some characters, the pronunciation of which is almost silent in particular words.

Some of these unique features can be explained by the fact that the Arabic script came to be used to write a language that evolved in the subcontinent, a long distance from where the script originated in the Middle East. How this came about is in turn related to the history of Muslim influence in the subcontinent and the evolution of languages and literary traditions in the places where Muslims settled in India and ruled from around the 14th until the 18th century. For Indian Muslims, Arabic maintained its importance as the sacred language of the Holy Quran and Persian continued to be an important spoken language as well as the language of administration and literary expression for much of this time. Over time a new language began to evolve, however, which was based on the dialect spoken in the north around Delhi but greatly influenced by Persian and Arabic. This influence came mostly in the form of the adoption of Arabic and Persian words and, eventually, the use of a modified form of the Persian script for writing purposes. In particular, new characters were added to this script to represent sounds that did not exist in Persian and Arabic and some of the distinctly Arabic and Persian sounds represented by particular characters were gradually diluted over time by speakers of this new language. The spellings of Persian and Arabic words have, however, remained faithful to the original. Hence the existence of different letters in the script representing the same sounds. The language that evolved, based on the dialect spoken in and around Delhi and enhanced by literary traditions in places such as Hyderabad in the south, came to be known as **rekhtā** ('mixed speech') as well as **zabān-e-urdū-e-mu'allā** ('the speech of the royal camps'). It was this second term which was finally abbreviated to provide Urdu with its modern name.

Many of the features of the Arabic script, and the anomalies that exist on account of its being applied to write Urdu, make learning to read and write this script a challenging task. It is for this reason that this book has been prepared. It is devoted entirely to the Urdu script rather than to the actual language, to give the student the opportunity to focus on learning to recognise the characters, both independently and when they occur in words. It is aimed at those with no previous knowledge of Urdu as well as those who can speak Urdu but cannot read or write it. The thirty-five characters are introduced gradually throughout the book and in an order that highlights those aspects of the script that are most likely to cause problems. Characters have not been introduced in the order in which they appear in the alphabet or in the conventional order in which they are taught. Rather, characters that are similar in shape have been deliberately spread over the chapters to focus attention on their differences rather than on their similarities. Because the book is also designed to help the student learn to write the characters, their formation is clearly detailed. There are also instructions on how to form whole words. These are designed to give the student a sense of the correct proportion of characters in relation to each other in a word and a feel for the flow of words when writing in Urdu. As far as possible, the words included in this book are generally common and it is hoped that this may assist the student in developing a reasonable vocabulary. This will be of use when he or she goes on to learn the language proper. Finally, a modified form of the Roman script has been used to indicate the pronunciation of particular sounds in Urdu. This means that some of the letters included are marked by macrons (¯) or tildes (˜), e.g. **ā**, **ẽ**, **ā̃**, or dots underneath. A macron indicates a long vowel, a tilde indicates that a vowel is pronounced through the nose and a dot under a consonant indicates that it is pronounced by placing the tip of the tongue on the roof of the mouth (e.g. **ḍ**, **ṭ**, **ṛ**). At the end of this introduction, all of the characters in the Urdu alphabet are provided, both in the order used in this book as well as their dictionary order. This will be a useful guide for quick reference while working through the chapters. Also included is a chart showing all of the other symbols that are explained and the chapter in which they first appear. There is also a reference section in which other useful materials for the study of Urdu are listed.

Several people have contributed to the production of this book and I would like to thank them for their time and efforts. I am particularly indebted to Jeananne Webber who read through the entire manuscript with great attention to detail; Rashid Sultan Sahib provided valuable comments and criticisms concerning the structure and content of the book; Belinda Greenwood-Smith, Ralph Saubern, John Robinson, Novi Djenar, Lidia Tanaka and Sudha Joshi all commented on various parts of the text and the Department of Asian Studies, La Trobe University, Bundoora, provided me with the facilities to complete this manuscript. I am also thankful to the students who have tested out these materials in various forms. I am solely responsible for all errors and inaccuracies.

Characters of the Urdu alphabet

Order used in this book

Unit	Name of character	Final form (unjoined)	Final form (joined)	Medial form	Initial form	Transliteration
1	**be**	ب	ـب	ـبـ	بـ	**b**
	kāf	ک	ـک	ـکـ	کـ	**k**
	lām	ل	ـل	ـلـ	لـ	**l**
	mīm	م	ـم	ـمـ	مـ	**m**
2	**alif**	ا	ـا	ـا	ا	**a, i, u, ā**
3	**pe**	پ	ـپ	ـپـ	پـ	**p**
	jīm	ج	ـج	ـجـ	جـ	**j**
	gāf	گ	ـگ	ـگـ	گـ	**g**
	choṭī he	ہ	ـہ	ـہـ	ہـ	**h**

4	**ye**	ی	ے / ی	ـیـ	یـ	**ī, e, ai, y**
5	**te**	ت	ـت	ـتـ	تـ	**t**
	cīm	چ	ـچ	ـچـ	چـ	**c**
	sīn	س	ـس	ـسـ	سـ	**s**
	nūn	ن	ـن	ـنـ	نـ	**n**
6	**vāo**	و	ـو	ـو	و	**ū, o, au, v**
7	**dāl**	د	ـد	ـد	د	**d**
	re	ر	ـر	ـر	ر	**r**
	baṛī he	ح	ـح	ـحـ	حـ	**h**
	shīn	ش	ـش	ـشـ	شـ	**sh**
	svād	ص	ـص	ـصـ	صـ	**s**
8	**zāl**	ذ	ـذ	ـذ	ذ	**z**
	ze	ز	ـز	ـز	ز	**z**
	khe	خ	ـخ	ـخـ	خـ	**kh**
	zād	ض	ـض	ـضـ	ضـ	**z**
	fe	ف	ـف	ـفـ	فـ	**f**
9	**ṭe**	ٹ	ـٹ	ـٹـ	ٹـ	**ṭ**
	ḍāl	ڈ	ـڈ	ـڈ	ڈ	**ḍ**
	ṛe	ڑ	ـڑ	ـڑ	ڑ	**ṛ**
	ghain	غ	ـغ	ـغـ	غـ	**gh**

	qāf	ق	ـق	ـقـ	قـ	**q**
10	**se**	ث	ـث	ـثـ	ثـ	**s**
	zhe	ژ	ـژ	ـژ	ژ	**z**
	to‘e	ط	ـط	ـطـ	طـ	**t**
	zo‘e	ظ	ـظ	ـظـ	ظـ	**z**
	‘ain	ع	ـع	ـعـ	عـ	**‘**

Other symbols

Unit	Symbol	Name	Description
1, 4	َ	**zabar**	indicates a short **a** vowel as well as the vowels **ai** and **au** when used with the characters ا **alif**, ی **ye** and و **vāo**.
1, 4	ِ	**zer**	denotes a short **i** vowel and is also used with the character ی **ye** to denote a long **ī** vowel. It is positioned under the character.
1, 5	ُ	**pesh**	denotes a short **u** vowel and is also used with the character و **vāo** to indicate a long **ū** vowel. It is positioned above the character.
1	ْ	**jasm**	indicates that a short vowel is not pronounced with a character. It is positioned above the character.
1	ّ	**tashdīd**	indicates that a character is repeated without an intervening

			vowel sound. It is positioned above the character.
2	ٓ	**madd**	placed above ا **alif** when in an initial position to represent the long vowel **ā**.
2	کا		irregular initial and medial forms of the character ک **kāf** with ا **alif** and ل **lām**.
3	ھ	**do cashmī he**	denotes that a character is aspirated (i.e. produced with a breath of air).
4	گا		irregular initial and medial forms of the character گ **gāf** with ا **alif** and ل **lām**.
11	ء	**hamzā**	indicates that one syllable in a word ends with a vowel and the next begins with one.

(m) or (f) after a noun indicates that it is respectively masculine or feminine.

Urdu alphabet in dictionary order

ا				
alif				
ب	پ	ت	ٹ	ث
be	**pe**	**te**	**ṭe**	**se**
ج	چ	ح	خ	
jīm	**cīm**	**baṛī he**	**<u>kh</u>e**	

د	ڈ	ذ	ر	ڑ	ز	ژ	
dāl	**ḍāl**	**zāl**	**re**	**ṛe**	**ze**	**zhe**	
س	ش	ص	ض	ط	ظ	ع	غ
sīn	**shīn**	**svād**	**zād**	**to'e**	**zo'e**	**'ain**	**ghain**
ف	ق	ک	گ	ل	م	ن	
fe	**qāf**	**kāf**	**gāf**	**lām**	**mīm**	**nūn**	
و	ہ	ی					
vāo	**choṭī he**	**ye**					

Vowel sounds in Urdu

There are ten vowel sounds in Urdu, three short and seven long vowels. The following chart shows the characters that are used to represent these sounds in particular positions in a word.

Vowel sound	Initial	Medial	Final
a (in ago)	ا **alif**	َ **zabar**	
i (in bit)	اِ **alif + zer**	ِ **zer**	
u (in put)	اُ **alif + pesh**	ُ **pesh**	
ī (in beet)	اِیـ **alif + ye + zer**	ـیِـ **ye + zer**	ی **ye**

e (bet)	ایـ	ـیـ	ے
	alif + ye	**ye**	**ye**
ai (in h**ay**)	اَیـ	ـَیـ	ے
	alif + ye+ zabar	**ye + zabar**	**ye**
ū (in f**oo**d)	اُو	ـُو	ـُو
	alif + vāo + pesh	**vāo + pesh**	**vāo + pesh**
o (in g**o**)	او	ـو	ـو
	alif + vāo	**vāo**	**vāo**
au (in l**or**d)	اَو	ـَو	ـَو
	alif + vāo + zabar	**vāo + zabar**	**vāo + zabar**

Useful reference materials

Barker, M. *et al., A Course in Urdu* (New York: Spoken Languages Service, 1990)

Barz, R. and Yadav, Y., *An Introduction to Hindi and Urdu* (Delhi: Munshiram Manoharlal, 1993)

Ferozsons Urdu English Dictionary: a comprehensive dictionary of current vocabulary (Lahore: Ferozsons Ltd, 1987)

Matthews, D. and Dalvi, M., *Teach Yourself Urdu* (London: Hodder & Stoughton,1999)

McGregor, R. S., *Outline of Hindi Grammar* (Oxford: Clarendon Press, 1987, second edn)

McGregor, R. S., *Urdu Study Materials* (Delhi: OUP, 1992)

McGregor, R. S. (ed.), *Oxford Hindi-English Dictionary* (Delhi: OUP, 1993)

Naim, C. M., Ahmad, Q.S., Nadvi, S.S., and Haq, M.A., *Introductory Urdu* (Chicago: Committee on South Asian Languages, University of Chicago, 1975)

Platts, J., *A Dictionary of Urdu, Classical Hindi and English* (London: OUP, 1960)

Russell, R., *A New Course in Urdu and Spoken Hindi* (London: School of Oriental and African Studies, London University, 1986)

Shackle, C. and Snell, R., *Hindi and Urdu since 1800: A Common Reader* (London: School of Oriental and African Studies, London University, 1990)

Zakir, M., *Lessons in Urdu Script* (Delhi: Idara-e-Amini, 1973)

UNIT 1

In the introduction we saw that the Urdu alphabet contains thirty-five characters, each of which has a name. When these characters are joined together to create words, the form of many changes depending on whether they appear at the beginning, in the middle or at the end of a word. The majority of characters join to both the preceding and the following character and, as a result, are known as **connecting characters**. Those that only join to the preceding character (but not to the following character) are called **non-connectors**. The four characters introduced in this unit are all connecting characters.

ب	ک	ل	م
be	**kāf**	**lām**	**mīm**

Pronunciation

These four characters represent consonant sounds.

Character	Name	Transliteration	Pronunciation
ب	**be**	**b**	b in **b**in
ک	**kāf**	**k**	k in s**k**ip
ل	**lām**	**l**	l in **l**ong
م	**mīm**	**m**	m in **m**an

Positional forms

The shapes of each of these characters vary in four ways depending on their position in a word. Remember that the following table should be read from right to left.

Name	Final form (unjoined)	Final form (joined)	Medial form	Initial form	Transliteration
be	ب	ـب	ـبـ	بـ	**b**
kāf	ک	ـک	ـکـ	کـ	**k**
lām	ل	ـل	ـلـ	لـ	**l**
mīm	م	ـم	ـمـ	مـ	**m**

☑ Writing practice

Each of the characters in the Urdu alphabet is formed in a precise manner and it is important to copy this exactly. Practise drawing the various forms of these four characters, following closely the guidelines given.

ب **be**

initial form

medial form

final form (joined)

final form (unjoined)

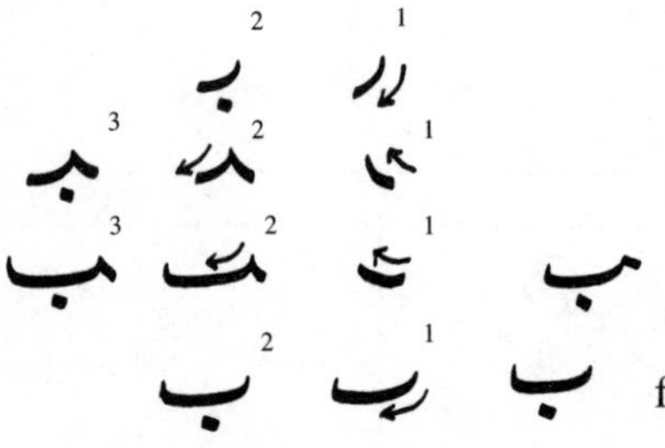

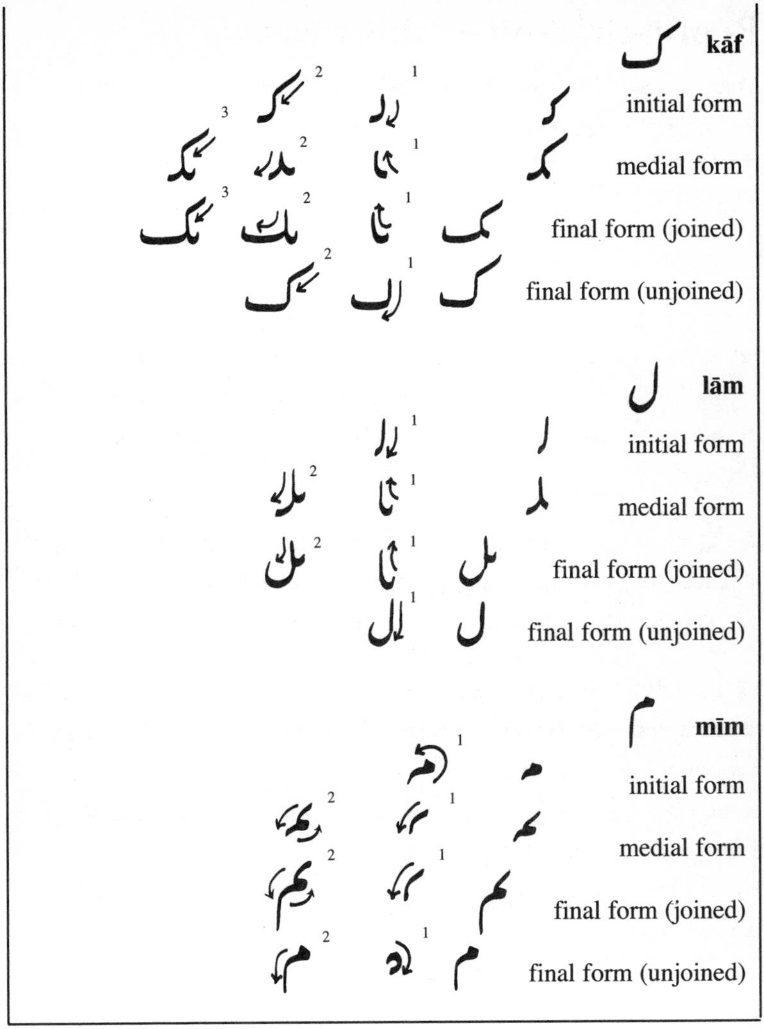
ک kāf
1 2 3
initial form
medial form
final form (joined)
final form (unjoined)
ل lām
initial form
medial form
final form (joined)
final form (unjoined)
م mīm
initial form
medial form
final form (joined)
final form (unjoined)

Representation of short vowels

There are no characters in the Urdu script representing the three short vowels in the language. These vowels are:

a in **a**go*

i in h**i**t

u in p**u**t

*It is important to remember that while the Roman letter **a** may represent several different sounds in English (e.g. in the words **ago**, **ate**, **arson**, **authority** and **ban**), it is used in this book to represent a single sound in Urdu.

These short vowels can be pronounced with all of the characters in the alphabet appearing anywhere in a word, except at the end. Two characters can also occur anywhere in a word without an intervening vowel sound.

Because there are no characters to represent the short vowels, it is difficult to tell which short vowel, if any, should be pronounced with a consonant character. There are, however, symbols that are employed, chiefly in dictionaries and children's primers, to clarify the pronunciation of words. These symbols represent the three short vowels and the omission of a vowel. These four symbols, written above and below characters, also possess names. They are:

◌َ	**zabar** (written above the character) = **a**
◌ِ	**zer** (written below the character) = **i**
◌ُ	**pesh** (written above the character) = **u**
◌ْ	**jazm** (written above the character) = no vowel*

*In some texts **jazm** appears as ° or ^ .

These symbols, however, are not used in most Urdu texts except where the pronunciation of a word needs clarification. In this book only the symbols ِ **zer**, ُ **pesh**, indicating the short **i** and **u**, and ْ **jazm** are provided. ْ **jazm** is, however, never written above the final character in a word because, as a rule, a short vowel cannot be pronounced in this position. Where ِ **zer** or ُ **pesh** are not provided in a word, it is to be assumed that the character is followed by a short **a** vowel. For example, the pronunciation of three words made up of the initial form of the character ب **be** and the final form of the character ک **kāf** is clarified in the following manner:

بک	بِک	بُک
bak	**bik**	**buk**
nonsense (f)	stem of the verb 'to be sold'	book (f)

Reading and writing practice

1. Read the following words in Urdu and write them in Roman script. Remember that the short vowels **i** and **u** are marked by ِ **zer** and ُ **pesh**, that the absence of a vowel symbol indicates the presence of a short **a** vowel and that a short vowel is not pronounced at the end of a word.

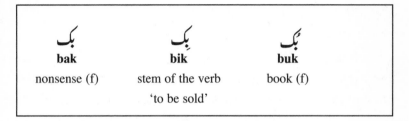

Meaning	Roman	Urdu
strength (m)		بل (a
lip (m)		لب (b
mill (m)		مِل (c
less		کم (d

when	کب	(e
book (f)	بُک	(f

2. Practise forming these words according to the guidelines given.

Meaning	4	3	2	1	
strength (m)		بل	بل	بـ	(a
lip (m)		لب	لب	لـ	(b
mill (m)		مل	مـا	مـ	(c
less		کم	لم	لـ	(d
when	کب	کـب	لب	لـ	(e
book (f)	بک	ـک	بلـ	بـ	(f

3. Connect the appropriate forms of the following characters to form the words. Remember to write in the short vowel symbols ِ **zer** and ُ **pesh** and the symbol ْ **jasm**, used to denote the omission of a vowel, where necessary.

	Roman	Meaning
م + ل + ک =	**mulk**	country (m) (a
ک + م + ل =	**kamal**	lotus (m) (b
ک + م + ب + ل =	**kambal**	blanket (m) (c
ب + ل + ب + ل =	**bulbul**	nightingale (m) (d

Summary

- The forms of most characters vary depending on whether they occur at the beginning, in the middle, at the end of a word or at the end after a non-connector.
- Each character has a name as well as a basic pronunciation.
- There are no characters to represent the three short vowels (**a**, **i**, **u**) in Urdu.
- There are four symbols occasionally employed to indicate the presence of a short vowel or the omission of a vowel (ـَ **zabar**, ـِ **zer**, ـُ **pesh** and ـْ **jazm**).
- Only the symbols ـِ **zer** and ـُ **pesh** are used in this book to represent short vowels.

Answers to practices

1. a) **bal** b) **lab** c) **mil** d) **kam** e) **kab** f) **buk**

3. a) مُلک b) کمل c) کُمبل d) بُلبُل

2 UNIT 2

In this chapter the first non-connecting character is introduced. It is also the first character in the Urdu alphabet and represents four vowel sounds.

ا **alif**

Positional forms

Non-connecting characters such as ا **alif** have only two forms, both of which are easy to recognise and draw.

Name	Final (joined) and medial form	Initial and final form (unjoined)	Transliteration
ا **alif**	ـا	ا	**ā, a, i, u**

Pronunciation

The pronunciation of ا **alif** depends on its position in a word.

Initial ا alif

In the absence of characters to represent the three short vowels in Urdu, ا **alif** is employed at the beginning of a word to indicate that it begins with one of these vowels. Occasionally the vowel symbols introduced in Unit 1 (َ **zabar**, ِ **zer** and ُ **pesh**) are used to clarify which of these vowels is present. In this book only the symbols for the short vowel **i**

(ـِ **zer**) and **u** (ـُ **pesh**) are written in. An initial short **a** vowel is thus indicated by ا **alif** without a vowel symbol.

For example:

اب	اِب	اُب
ab	**ib**	**ub**

Initial ا alif with the symbol ~ madd

ا **alif** also represents a long **ā** vowel at the beginning of a word. When it does, the symbol ~ **madd** is written (from right to left) above it.

Character	Name	Transliteration	Pronunciation
آ	**alif** and **madd**	**ā***	**a** in father

*The line above this letter in the Roman is used to distinguish this vowel sound from the short **a** (in **a**go) vowel introduced in Unit 1.

Medial ا alif

In the middle of a word ا **alif** represents a long **ā** vowel.

Character	Name	Transliteration	Pronunciation
ا	**alif**	**ā**	**a** in father

For example:

اب	اِب	اُب	آب	با
ab	**ib**	**ub**	**āb**	**bā**

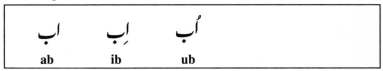

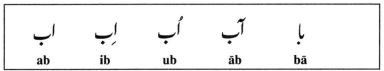

Modified form of ک kāf

The initial and medial forms of ک **kāf** are written in a modified form when they are followed by either ا **alif** or ل **lām**.

For example:

کا	=	ا	+	ک	کل	=	ل	+	ک
kā		**alif**		**kāf**	**kal**		**lām**		**kāf**
's					yesterday/tomorrow				

ّ tashdīd

The symbol ّ **tashdīd**, which looks very much like the letter **w**, represents the doubling of a character without an intervening vowel sound. It is written above the character that is repeated.

For example:

اِکّا

ikkā

a one-horse vehicle (m)

☑ Reading and writing practice

1. Practise forming the following words according to the guidelines given.

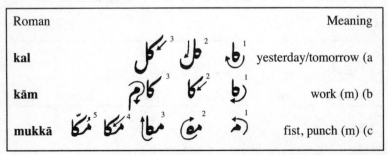

Roman	Meaning
kal	yesterday/tomorrow (a
kām	work (m) (b
mukkā	fist, punch (m) (c

2. Join the appropriate forms of the following characters.

Roman		Urdu
bā	= ا + بـ	(a
kā	= ا + کـ	(b
lā	= ا + لـ	(c
mā	= ا + مـ	(d

3. Read the following words and write them in Roman script.

Meaning	Roman	Urdu	
lotus (m)		کمل	(a
hair (m)		بال	(b
red		لال	(c
tall, long		لُمبا	(d
Muslim spiritual guide (m)		اِمام	(e
black		کالا	(f
collection of poetry (m)		کلام	(g
bomb (m)		بم	(h
mango (m)		آم	(i
goods (m)		مال	(j

Meaning	Roman	Urdu	
maternal uncle (m)		ماما	(k
a woman's name (f)		کُملا	(l
complete		مُکمّل	(m

4. Join the appropriate forms of the following characters to form the words given. Also write in the words any necessary short vowels symbols and ْ **jazm** (omission of vowel).

	Roman	Meaning	
آ + ب =	**āb**	water (m)	(a
ا + ب =	**ab**	now	(b
ل + ا + م =	**lām**	name of a character	(c
ک + ا + م =	**kām**	work (m)	(d
ب + ل + ا =	**balā**	calamity (f)	(e
ک + ل + ا =	**kalā**	art (f)	(f
ب + ا + ل + ا =	**bālā**	high, above	(g
م + ا + ل + ا =	**mālā**	necklace (f)	(h

	Roman	Meaning
ل + ا + ل + ا =	**lālā**	honorific title (i
ک + م + ا + ل =	**kamāl**	miracle (m) (j
ک + ل + ا + ک =	**klāk**	clock (m) (k
ا + ب + ا =	**abbā**	father (m) (l

5. Read the following phrases in Urdu and then write them in Roman script.

Meaning	Roman	Urdu
black blanket (m)		کالا کُمبل (a
red lotus (m)		لال کمل (b
complete work (m)		مُکمّل کام (c
less work (m)		کم کام (d
a long hair (m)		لُمبا بال (e
yesterday/ tomorrow's work (m)		کل کا کام (f
uncle's miracle (m)		ماما کا کمال (g

the Imam's work (m)	اِمام کا کام (h
father's mango (m)	ابّا کا آم (i

Summary

- ا **alif** is a non-connector (i.e. does not join to the following character).
- ا **alif** is used to indicate a short vowel (**a**, **i**, **u**) at the beginning of a word.
- ا **alif** with ~ **madd** at the beginning of a word represent the long vowel **ā**.
- ا **alif** in the middle of a word also represents the long vowel **ā**.
- The form of the character ک **kāf** is modified when followed by ا **alif** or ل **lām.**
- The doubling of a character without an intervening vowel is represented by the symbol ّ **tashdīd**, written above the character.

Answers to practices

2. a) با b) کا c) لا d) ما

3. a) **kamal** b) **bāl** c) **lāl** d) **lambā** e) **imām** f) **kālā** g) **kalām** h) **bam** i) **ām** j) **māl** k) **māmā** l) **kamlā** m) **mukammal**

4. a) آب b) اب c) لام d) کام e) بلا f) کلا
g) بالا h) مالا i) لالا j) کمال k) کُلّاک l) ابّا

5. a) **kālā kambal** b) **lāl kamal** c) **mukammal kām** d) **kam kām** e) **lambā bāl** f) **kal kā kām** g) **māmā kā kamāl** h) **imām kā kām** i) **abbā kā ām**

3 UNIT 3

The four characters introduced in this unit are all connecting characters representing consonant sounds. In addition to these, the symbol that represents aspiration (i.e. a breath of air expelled with a character) is described. The four characters are:

پ	ج	گ	ہ
pe	**jīm**	**gāf**	**choṭī he**

Pronunciation

Character	Name	Transliteration	Pronunciation
پ	**pe**	**p**	**p** in s**p**in
ج	**jīm**	**j**	**j** in **j**ump
گ	**gāf**	**g**	**g** in **g**un (never as in **g**in)
ہ	**choṭī he**	**h**	**h** in **h**ut

In some words a short **a** vowel followed by ہ **choṭī he** at the end of a word are pronounced together as a long **ā** vowel. They are also occasionally pronounced as a short **i** or **e** vowel. Where such words are introduced in this book, first the Roman transliteration is given and then the pronunciation in parentheses.

For example:

کلمہ
kalmah *
(kalmā)
the expression of faith of a Muslim (m) ('there is no God but Allah...')

*See below for the final form of ہ **choṭī he**.

Positional forms

Being connectors, all of these characters have four forms. پ **pe** and گ **gāf** have the same basic shape as the characters ب **be** and ک **kāf**, introduced in Unit 1. Because of this similarity both sets of characters are traditionally considered part of the same series in the Urdu alphabet.

Name	Final form (unjoined)	Final form (joined)	Medial form	Initial form	Transliteration
pe	پ	ـپ	ـپـ	پـ	**p**
jīm	ج	ـج	ـجـ	جـ	**j**
gāf	گ	ـگ	ـگـ	گـ	**g**
choṭī he	ہ	ـہ	ـہـ	ہـ	**h**

☑ Writing practice

Practise drawing the various forms of the four characters introduced in this unit according to the guidelines given.

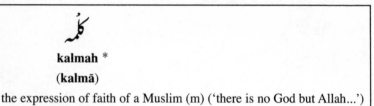

پ **pe**

For a description of how to draw the character پ **pe**, see the formation of ب **be** on p.2.

ج **jīm**

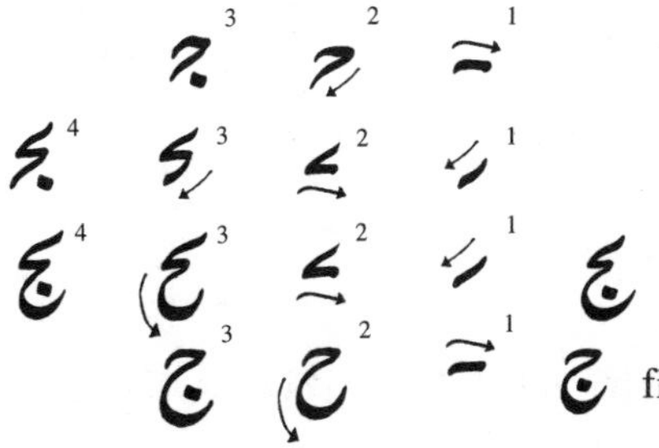

initial form

medial form

final form (joined)

final form (unjoined)

گ **gāf**

For a description of how to draw the character گ **gāf**, see the formation of ک **kāf** on p.3. The second stroke at the top of the character is drawn the same way as the first, i.e. downwards.

ہ **choṭī he**

There are two initial forms of the character **choṭī he**: ہ **choṭī he** when joined to ا **alif** and when joined to any other character.

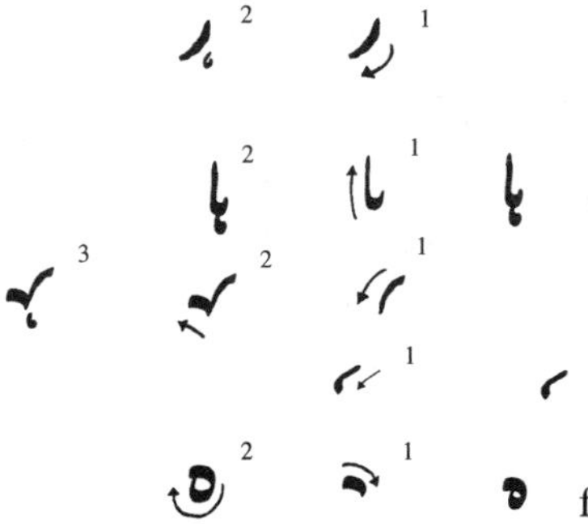

initial form

initial form (followed by ا **alif**)

medial form

final form (joined)

final form (unjoined)

Modified form of گ gāf

As with ک **kāf**, the initial and medial forms of the character گ **gāf** also appear in a modified form when followed by either ا **alif** or ل **lām**.

For example:

گا	=	ا	+	گ	گُل	=	ل	+	گ
gā		**alif**		**gāf**	**gul**		**lām**		**gāf**
stem of the verb to sing					flower (m)				

☑ Reading and writing practice

1. Read the following words and then write them in Roman script.

Meaning	Roman	Urdu	
you (polite)		آپ	(a
today		آج	(b
fire (f)		آگ	(c
a sigh (f)		آہ	(d

2. Practise forming the following words according to the guidelines and then write them in Roman script. Note that any dots are added to a portion of a word after writing a non-connecting character. For example, in the first word the three dots that complete the character پ **pe** are added after drawing ا **alif** but before beginning the character ک **kāf**. If more than one character with dots occurs in a word, the dots are completed from right to left.

Roman		Meaning
	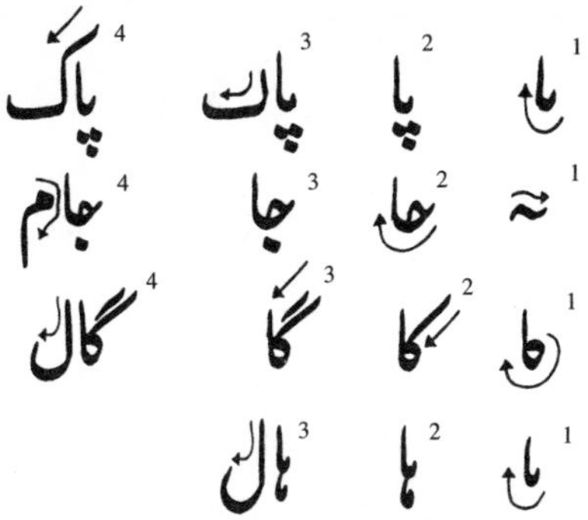	pure (a
		drinking vessel (m) (b
		cheek (m) (c
		hall (m) (d

3. Join the appropriate forms of the following characters to form the words given.

		Roman	Meaning
=	ل + پ + ک	**lapak**	leap (f) (a
=	ب + ج + ا	**bajā**	chimed (b
=	ل + گ + ا	**lagā**	attached (c
=	ک + ہ + ا	**kahā**	said (d

4. Write out the full (unjoined final) forms of the characters that make up the following words and then provide their Roman equivalents.

Roman					Meaning
		+	=	گپ	gossip (f) (a
		+	=	جج	judge (m) (b
		+	=	جگ	world (m) (c
	+	+	=	جگہ	place (f) (d

5. Select the appropriate forms of the characters provided and then join them to make the following words.

	Roman	Meaning
= ا + ل + م + گ	**gamlā**	flower pot (m) (a
= ل + گ + ا + پ	**pāgal**	crazy (b
= م + ا + گ + ل	**lagām**	reins (f) (c
= ک + ل + ب + پ	**pablik**	public (d
= ج + ا + ج + ب	**bajāj**	brand name of a scooter (e
= پ + ا + پ	**pāp**	sin (m) (f

	Roman	Meaning
ہ + ل + ک + ا =	**halkā**	light (g
ہ + ل + ا + ک =	**halāk**	killed (h
گ + ل + ا =	**galā**	throat (m) (i
ک + ل + ا =	**kalā**	art (f) (j

Aspiration

A particular form of the character ہ **choṭī he** is also employed to indicate that a consonant character is pronounced with a breath of air (i.e. aspiration). An example of an aspirated consonant in English is the initial **p** in the word **pit**. Place your open palm approximately ten centimetres from your mouth and pronounce both **pit** and **spit**. Can you feel the breath of air which is expelled with the first **p?** The form of ہ **choṭī he** that indicates aspiration is called **do cashmī he**.

Pronunciation

Character	Name	Transliteration	Pronunciation
ھ	**do cashmī he**	**h**	a breath of air expelled with a consonant

Writing practice

Practise forming the character **do cashmī he** according to the guidelines given.

do cashmī he

Reading and writing practice

6. Write the following forms in Roman script.

(a با (b پا (c جا (d کا (e گا

Roman

(f بھا (g پھا (h جھا (i کھا (j گھا

Roman

7. Practise forming the following words according to the guidelines given.

	Roman	Meaning
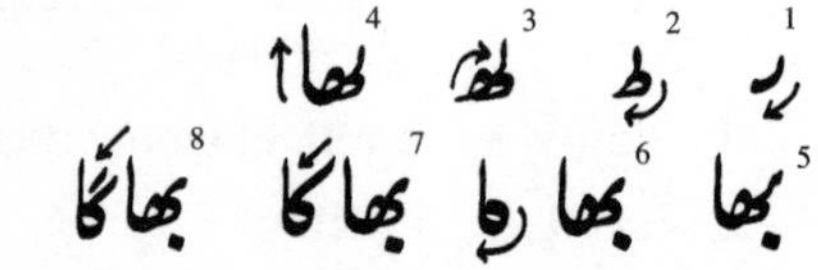	**bhāgā**	fled (a
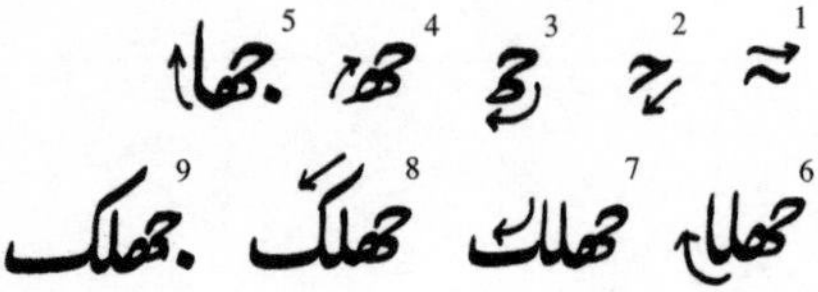	**jhalak**	glimpse (f) (b

Roman	Meaning
phal	fruit (m) (c
khāl	skin (f) (d

Summary

- The characters پ **pe** and گ **gāf** have the same basic form as the characters ب **be** and ک **kāf**, introduced in Unit 1.
- Dots are added last or after a non-connecting character. If there is more than one character with dots in a word, they are added from right to left.
- There are two forms of the character ہ **choṭī he** in an initial position: ہ **choṭī he** with ا **alif** and ہ **choṭī he** with any other character.
- The character گ **gāf** has a modified form before ا **alif** or ل **lām**.
- A particular form of ہ **choṭī he** called **do cashmī he** ھ is used to indicate that a consonant character is aspirated (i.e. produced with a breath of air).
- Occasionally a short **a** vowel followed by ہ **choṭī he** in a word final position is pronounced as a long **ā** vowel.

Answers to practices

1. a) **āp** b) **āj** c) **āg** d) **āh**

2. a) **pāk** b) **jām** c) **gāl** d)**hāl**

3. a) لپک b) بجا c) لگا d) کہا

4. a) گ پ **gap** b) ج ج **jaj**
   c) ج گ **jag** d) ج گ ہ **jagah**

5. a) گملہ b) پاگل c) لگام d) پبلک
   e) بجاج f) پاپ g) ہلکا h) ہلاک
   i) گلا j) کلا

6. a) **bā** b) **pā** c) **jā** d) **kā** e) **gā** f) **bhā** g) **phā** h) **jhā** i) **khā** j) **ghā**

4 UNIT 4

Only one character is introduced in this unit. It is a connector and represents three long vowels and the semi-vowel **y**.

ی **ye**

Positional forms

The basic shape of the initial and medial forms of the character ی **ye** is the same as that of ب **be** and پ **pe**, introduced in early units. This character also has two final forms, both of which represent separate vowel sounds.

Name	Final form (unjoined)	Final form (joined)	Medial form	Initial form	Transliteration
ye	ے ی	ے ی	ـیـ	یـ	**ī, e, ai, y**

☑ Writing practice

Practise drawing the various forms of this character according to the guidelines given.

ی ye

یـ initial form

ـیـ medial form

ی final form (joined) (ī)

ے final form (joined) (**e, ai**)

ی final form (unjoined) (ī)

ے final form (unjoined) (**e, ai**)

Pronunciation

The character ی **ye** represents three long vowels and the semi-vowel **y**.

Character	Name	Transliteration	Pronunciation
ی	**ye**	**y** **ī** **e** **ai**	**y** in **yes** **ī** in b**ee**t **e** in pl**ay** **ai** in h**a**d

Word-initial ی ye

At the beginning of a word, ی **ye** represents the semi-vowel **y**.

For example:

یا	یہ
yā	**yah**
	(ye)*
or	this, he, she, it, they

*The pronunciation of this word is exceptional. See the explanation of the pronunciation of ہ **choṭī he** at the end of a word in Unit 3 (p.15).

Initial ī, e, ai vowels

When a long **ī**, **e**, or **ai** vowel occurs at the beginning of a word, it is represented by ی **ye**, preceded by the character ا **alif**. Occasionally the vowel symbol َ **zabar** is employed to indicate that it represents **ai** and ِ **zer** to indicate that it represents **ī**. The absence of these two vowel-markers thus indicates the presence of the vowel **e**.

اِیکھ	ایک	اَیسا
īkh	**ek**	**aisā***
sugarcane (f)	one	such/thus(f)

* سـ is the medial form of the character س **sīn**, which represents the consonant **s**. This is introduced in Unit 5.

Medial ی ye

In the middle of a word ی **ye** may represent any one of the three long vowels and the semi-vowel **y**. Once again the vowel symbols َ **zabar** and ِ **zer** are occasionally used to indicate which of these sounds is present. When ی **ye** is followed by ا **alif**, it frequently represents the semi-vowel **y** or **iy** or even **īy**.

پیلا	کیلا	بَیل	بیاہ	کیا	کِیا	ایّام
pīlā	**kelā**	**bail**	**byāh**	**kyā**	**kiyā**	**ayyām**
yellow	banana (m)	ox (m)	marriage (m)	what	did	days (m)

Word-final ی ye

There are two forms of ی **ye** when it occurs at the end of a word: ی (**ī**) and ے (**e, ai**).

For example:

بے	ہے	جی
be	**hai**	**jī**
without (prefix)	is/are	heart/mind (also a polite suffix)

☑ Reading and writing practice

1. Follow the steps to form the following words and then write them out in Roman script.

Roman	Meaning
	jalebi (m) (a (an Indian sweet)
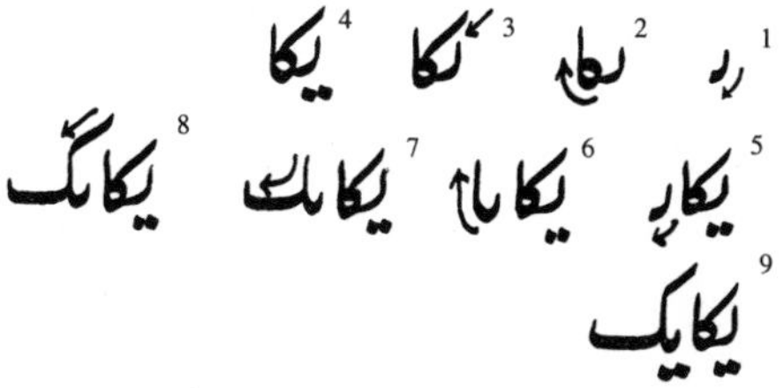	suddenly (b
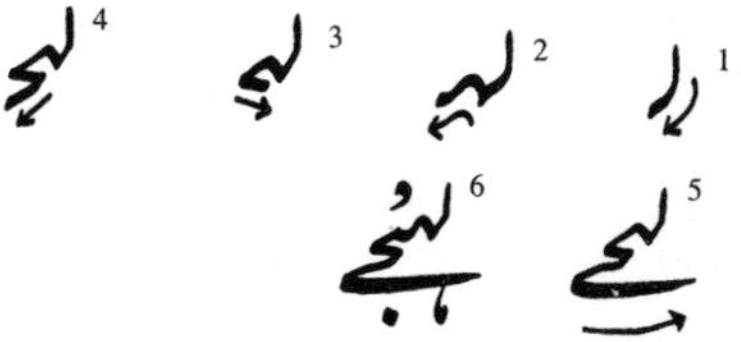	accents (m) (c

2. Read the following words and write them in Roman script.

Meaning	Roman	Urdu
even, also		بھی (a
drunk, drink		پی (b
take		لے (c
is/are		ہے (d
ghee (m) (clarified butter)		گھی (e
’s		کے (f

3. Write the following words employing the appropriate forms of the characters supplied.

	Roman	Meaning
پ + ی + ل + ا =	**pīlā**	yellow (a
ک + ب + ھ + ی =	**kabhī**	sometimes (b
ک + ھ + ا + ی + ا =	**khāyā**	eaten (c
ا + ی + ک =	**ek**	one (d

4. Read the following words quickly, focusing on the differences that separate them, and then write them in Roman script.

بھلا	بلا	بالا	بال	بل	(a
good	calamity (f)	above	hair (m)	strength (m)	
پھل	پلا	پالا	پال	پُل	(b
fruit (m)	reared	nurtured	a sail (m)	bridge (m)	
جھلا جھل	جلا	جالا	جال	جل	(c
shining	burnt	cobweb (m)	net (m)	water (m)	
کھال	کلا	کالا	کال	کل	(d
skin (f)	art (f)	black	period (m)	yesterday	

گلا	گالا	گال	گُل	(e
throat (m)	cotton ball (m)	cheek (m)	flower (m)	

گِیلا	پیلا	جیل	کھیل	لَیمپ	کیلا	(f
wet	yellow	jail (m/f)	game (m)	lamp (m)	banana (m)	

Punctuation

The most important punctuation marks used in Urdu sentences are as follows:

؟	=	?
۔	=	.
،	=	,
؛	=	;

Other punctuation marks are the same as the English.

☑ Reading and writing practice

5. It is now possible to read one or two sentences using some of the words you have learnt already. Try and read the following sentences and write them out in Roman script. It will help to know that the verb generally comes at the end of the sentence in Urdu. (The words in parentheses show the Urdu word order.)

(a یہ کُیا ہَے؟

Roman

(is what this)

What is this?

(b یہ ایک پھل ہَے۔

Roman

(is fruit one this)

This is a fruit.

(c کُیا یہ آپ کی جلیبی ہَے؟

Roman

(is jalebi your this)

Is this your jalebi?

(d یہ پُیالا پِیلا ہَے۔

Roman

(is yellow cup this)

This cup is yellow.

(e کیا یہ آپ کی گلی ہَے؟

Roman

(is alley your this)

Is this your alley?

(f آپ کا پیالا پِیلا ہَے۔

Roman

(is yellow cup your)

Your cup is yellow.

Summary

- The character ی **ye** represents three long vowels (**ī**, **e**, **ai**) and the semi-vowel **y**.
- ی **ye** has two final forms ی (**ī**) and ے (**e**, **ai**).
- At the beginning of a word the long vowels **ī**, **e** and **ai** are represented by ا **alif** and ی **ye**.
- The vowel symbol ِ **zer** is employed to mark that the character ی **ye** represents the vowel **ī** while the vowel symbol َ **zabar** is employed to mark that it represents **ai**.
- The pronunciation of the pronoun یہ **yah** (**ye**) (he, she, it, this, they) is irregular.
- ؟ = ?

  ۔ = .

  ، = ,

  ؛ = ;

Answers to practices

1. a) **jalebī** b) **yakāyak** c) **lahje (lehje)**

2. a) **bhī** b) **pī** c) **le** d) **hai** e) **ghī** f) **ke**

3. a) پیلا b) کبھی c) کھایا d) ایک

4. a) **bal, bāl, bālā, balā, bhalā** b) **pul, pāl, pālā, palā, phal** c) **jal, jāl, jālā, jalā, jhalā jhal** d) **kal, kāl, kālā, kalā, khāl** e) **gul, gāl, gālā, galā** f) **kelā, laimp, khel, jel, pīlā, gīlā**

5. a) **yah (ye) kyā hai?** b) **yah (ye) ek phal hai** c) **kyā yah (ye) āp kī jalebī hai?** d) **yah (ye) pyālā pīlā hai** e) **kyā yah (ye) āp kī galī hai?** f) **āp kā pyālā pīlā hai**

5 UNIT 5

In this unit four connecting characters are introduced, one of which is also used to represent the nasalisation of a vowel. These characters are:

ت	چ	س	ن
te	**cīm**	**sīn**	**nūn**

Pronunciation

All four of these characters represent consonant sounds.

Character	Name	Transliteration	Pronunciation
ت	**te**	**t**	**t** in **t**on (the tip of the tongue touches the back of the top teeth)
چ	**cīm**	**c**	**ch** in **ch**urch (never the c in **c**at)*
س	**sīn**	**s**	**s** in **s**un
ن	**nūn**	**n**	**n** in **n**ut

*Note that the sound **ch** is represented in the Roman by the letter **c** in this book. This is because there is an aspirated form of چ **cīm**, which is represented in Roman script by **ch**.

Positional forms

The basic form of the character ت **te** is the same as that of ب **be** and پ **pe**. The shape of چ **cīm** is also identical to that of ج **jīm**, introduced in Unit 3. In both cases it is only the number of dots that differs.

Name	Final form (unjoined)	Final form (joined)	Medial form	Initial form	Transliteration
te	ت	ـت	ـتـ	تـ	**t**
cīm	چ	ـچ	ـچـ	چـ	**c**
sīn	س	ـس	ـسـ	سـ	**s**
nūn	ن	ـن	ـنـ	نـ	**n**

☑ Writing practice

Practise forming these new characters according to the guidelines given.

ت **te**

For a description of how to draw the character ت **te**, see the formation of ب **be** on p. 2.

چ **cīm**

For a description of how to draw the character چ **cīm**, see the formation of ج **jīm** on p.17.

س sīn

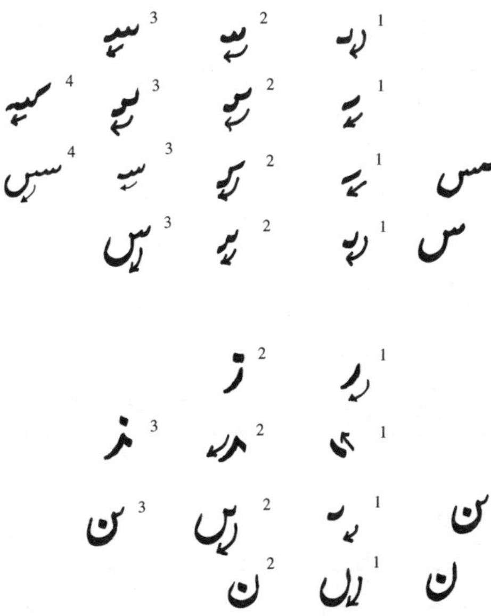

سـ initial form

ـسـ medial form

ـس final form (joined)

س final form (unjoined)

ن nūn

نـ initial form

ـنـ medial form

ـن final form (joined)

ن final form (unjoined)

Reading and writing practice

1. Practise forming the following words according to the guidelines given.

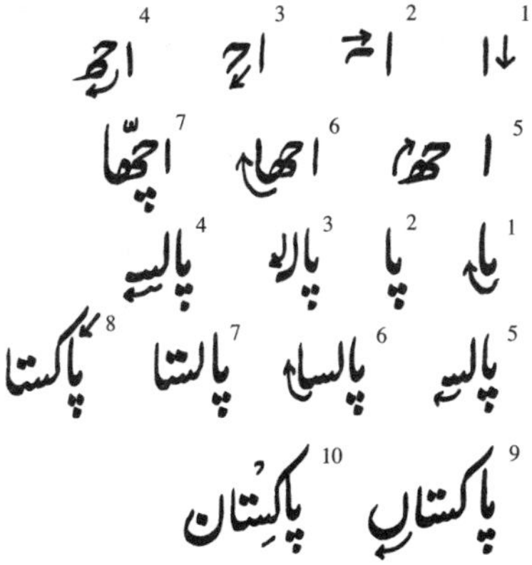

Roman	Meaning
acchā	good, okay (a
pakistān	Pakistan (m) (b

	Roman	Meaning
	**kuch**	some, something (c
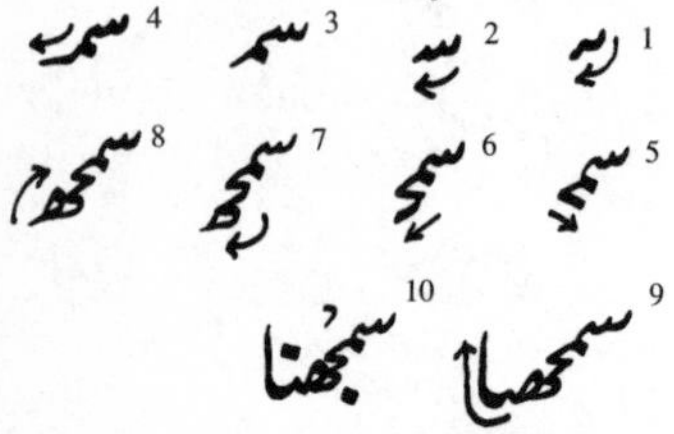	**samajhnā**	to understand (d

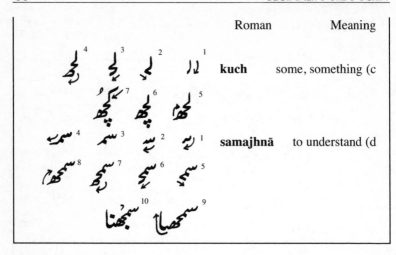

2. Read the following words and write them in Roman script.

Meaning	Roman	Urdu
hand (m)		ہاتھ (a
conversation (f)		بات چِیت (b
smile (f)		مُسکان (c
from		سے (d
settlement (f)		بُستی (e

3. Join the appropriate forms of the following characters to form the words given.

	Roman	Meaning
ت + ی + ل =	**tel**	a) oil (m)
ن + ا + م =	**nām**	b) name (m)
چ + م + ک =	**camak**	c) shine (f)
س + ا + ل =	**sāl**	d) year (m)

4. Complete the following words by placing the correct number of dots above or below the appropriate character.

ٮھی	d)	ٮاک	c)	ٮھا	b)	ٮا	a)
bhī also/even		**nāk** nose (f)		**thā** was		**yā** or	
حھٮکلی	h)	حھلک	g)	حالاک	f)	ٮاس	e)
cipkalī lizard (f)		**jhalak** glimpse (f)		**cālāk** shrewd		**pās** near	

5. Read the following words and write them in Roman script.

Meaning	Roman	Urdu	
statement (m)		بیان	(a
to tell		بتانا	(b
to save		بچانا	(c
to ring, strike		بجانا	(d
heard		سُنا	(e
assembly (f)		سبھا	(f
Tuesday (m)		منگل	(g
jungle (m)		جنگل	(h
such		اَیسا	(i
how		کَیسا	(j

Nasalisation

The character ن **nūn** is also used to represent nasalisation (the pronunciation of a vowel sound partly through the nose) in Urdu. In the middle of a word the medial form of ن **nūn** is employed (ﻨ) while at the end of a word the final form of ن **nūn** is written without the dot when it represents a nasalised vowel, i.e. ں. This particular final form of ن **nūn** is called **nūn ghunnā** (lit: 'talking through the nose'). In this book, the nasalisation of vowel is represented in Roman script by a tilde (˜) written above a vowel, e.g. **ã**. When trying to determine whether the character **nūn** in a medial position represents the nasalisation of a vowel or the consonant **n**, it may help to remember that long vowels are often nasalised.

For example:

اِنْسان	آنکھ
insān	**ā̃kh**
human being (m)	eye (f)
مان	ماں
mān	**mā̃**
honour/respect (m)	mother (f)

Occasionally the final form of ن **nūn** without the dot, representing nasalisation, is found in the middle of a word.

For example:

لِکھیںگے or لِکھیں گے

likhẽge

he/they (m) will write

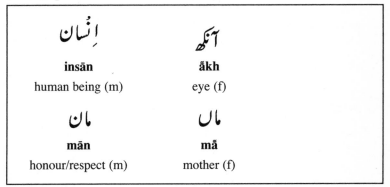

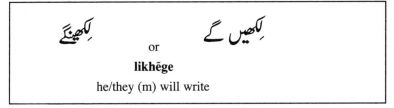

Nasalisation is a very common feature in Urdu. Two commonly used words that are nasalised are the words for **yes** and **no**:

جی ہاں	جی نہیں
jī hā̃	**jī nahī̃***
yes	no

*The word جی **jī** literally means heart or mind but is used here to soften the words and to add a degree of respect. It is also commonly used after people's names as a sign of respect.

☑ Reading and writing practice

6. Choose the appropriate forms of the following characters and form the words given.

	Roman	Meaning
م + ی + ں =	**mē̃**	in (a
ی + ہ + ا + ں =	**yahā̃**	here (b
	samjhē̃ge	will understand (c
س + م + ج + ھ + ی + ں + گ + ی =		

7. Read the following words and write them in Roman script.

Meaning	Roman	Urdu
where (?)		کہاں (a
(to) us		ہمیں (b
I		مَیں (c
(to) him/her/them		اُنہیں (d
books (f)		کِتابیں (e

8. Read the following words quickly and then write them in Roman script.

کِتنا	یکساں	تھکنا	(a
how much (?)	similar	to become tired	
بتّیس	کیتلی	کیلا	
thirty-two	kettle (f)	banana (n)	
بنانا	کمبل	کنگال	(b
to make	blanket (m)	destitute	
نتیجہ	بتلانا	نبی	
conclusion (m)	to tell	prophet (m)	

مجلس	جاپانی	چابی	(c
party (f)	Japanese	key (f)	
سچ مچ	سجانا	مچھلی	
really	to decorate	fish (f)	

Summary

- The character چ **cīm** is represented by the letter **c** in Roman script This is pronounced as **ch** in the word **ch**urch.
- The basic form of ت **te** is the same as that of ب **be** and پ **pe**.
- The tip of the tongue touches the back of the top teeth when pronouncing ت **te**.
- The form of چ **cīm** is the same as that of ج **jīm**.
- The initial and medial forms of ن **nūn** have the same basic shapes as those of the characters in the ب **be** series.
- The character ن **nūn** is also used to represent nasalisation in Urdu. In the middle of a word the medial form of ن **nūn** is employed (نـ) while at the end of a word the final form of ن **nūn** is written without the dot when it represents a nasalised vowel (ں).

Answers to practices

2. a) **hāth** b) **bāt cīt** c) **muskān** d) **se** e) **bastī**

3. a) تیل b) نام c) چمک d) سال

4. a) یا b) تھا c) ناک d) بھی

e) پاس f) چالاک g) جھلک h) چھپکلی

5. a) **bayān** b) **batānā** c) **bacānā** d) **bajānā** e) **sunā** f) **sabhā** g) **mangal** h) **jangal** i) **aisā** j) **kaisā**

6. a) میں b) یہاں c) سمجھینگے

7. a) **kahā̃** b) **hamẽ** c) **maĩ** d) **unhẽ** e) **kitābẽ**

8. a) **thaknā**, **yaksā̃**, **kitnā**, **kelā**, **ketlī**, **battīs** b) **kangāl**, **kambal**, **banānā**, **nabī**, **batlānā**, **natījah (natījā)** c) **cābī**, **jāpānī**, **majlīs**, **machlī**, **sajānā**, **sacmuc**

6 UNIT 6

In this unit the character و **vāo**, a non-connector that represents three long vowels and a semi-vowel, is introduced.

و **vāo**

Positional forms

Because it does not connect to the following character in a word, و **vāo**, like ا **alif**, has only two forms, both of which are almost identical in appearance and easily recognisable.

Name	Medial and final form (joined)	Initial and final form (unjoined)	Transliteration
vāo	ـو	و	**ū, o, au, v**

Writing practice

Practise writing the two forms of the character و **vāo** following the guidelines.

و **vāo**

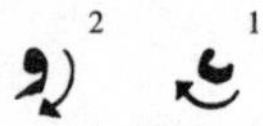 و initial and final form (unjoined)

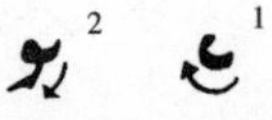 ـو medial and final form (joined)

Pronunciation

The character و **vāo** may represent three vowel sounds and the semi-vowel **v**.

Character	Name	Transliteration	Pronunciation
و	**vāo**	**v**	somewhere between the English **v** and **w**. The upper teeth make slight contact with the back of the lower lip
		ū	**ū** in f**oo**d
		o	**o** in g**o** (without the **w** sound at the end)
		au	**au** in l**or**d

Word-initial و vāo

At the beginning of a word, و **vāo** represents the semi-vowel **v**.
For example:

وجہ	وہاں
vajah	**vahā̃**
reason	there

Initial ū, o, au vowels

The presence of one of the long vowels **ū**, **o**, **au** at the beginning of a word is marked by ا **alif** followed by و **vāo**. This combination of characters may, however, also represent a short vowel and the semi-vowel **v**. The vowels **ū** and **au** are occasionally distinguished using the short vowel-markers َ **zabar** (**au**) and ُ **pesh** (**ū**). This practice has been followed in this book.

For example:

اُون	اولے	اَور	اوّل
ūn	**ole**	**aur***	**avval**
wool (n)	hailstones (n)	and	first, chief, best

*The final character in this word is the independent form of the character ر **re**, which represents the consonant **r**.

Medial و vāo

In the middle of a word و **vāo** generally represents one of the three long vowels just described. Again, the short vowel signs may be employed to clarify which vowel is present. When و **vāo** is followed by either ا **alif** or ی **ye**, it often represents the semi-vowel **v**.

For example:

تُو	تو	سَو	سوال	نوِیس
tū	**to**	**sau**	**savāl**	**navīs**
you	then	one hundred	question (n)	writer/scribe

☑ Reading and writing practice

1. Following the guidelines given, write out these words. After you have done this, write their Roman equivalents.

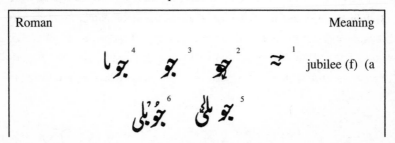

Roman		Meaning
	جوبا ⁴ جو ³ جو ² جـ ¹	jubilee (f) (a
	جُوبلی ⁶ جوبلی ⁵	

Roman		Meaning
	1 جـ 2 جا 3 جا 4 جاس 5 جاسو 6 جاسو 7 جاسوس 8 جاسُوس	spy (m) (b
	1 بـ 2 بیـ 3 بیو 4 بیوی	wife (f) (c
	1 بو 2 بو 3 بوجـ 4 بوجـ 5 بوجھ 6 بوجھ 7 بوجھا 8 بوجھل 9 بوجھل	heavy (d

2. Read the following words and write them out in Roman script.

Meaning	Roman	Urdu
square (m)		چَوک (a
high		اُونچا (b
death (f)		مَوت (c
step-, half-*		سَوتیلا (d

*as in step-sister

3. Join the appropriate forms of the following characters to make the words given.

	Roman	Meaning
ج + و + ا + ن =	**javān**	youth (m) (a
چ + ا + و + ل =	**cāval**	rice (m) (b
س + م + و + س + ا =	**samosā**	samosa (m) (c
م + و + س + م =	**mausam**	weather (m) (d
س + و + ک + ھ + ن + ا =	**sūkhnā**	to dry (e
ک + ی + و + ں =	**kyõ**	why (?) (f

4. Write the full (unjoined final) forms of the characters that make up the following words.

	Roman	Meaning
مُسلمان = + + + + +	**musalmān**	Muslim (m) (a
مَولوی = + + + +	**maulvī**	learned man (m) (b
پینسِل = + + + +	**pensil**	pencil (m) (c
نَوجوان = + + + + + +	**nau javān**	young man (m) (d
ہسپتال = + + + + + +	**haspatāl**	hospital (m) (e

5. Read the following phrases and write them in Roman script. Note that words that appear with vowel-markers (َ **zabar**, ِ **zer** and ُ **pesh**) or ْ **jasm** reappear without these symbols. This is designed to assist in recognising words as they would appear in unedited texts.

(a	آپ کی کِتاب your book	لال کتاب red book	
	Roman		
(b	نَوجوان کی کتاب the youth's book	نوجوان کا سامان the youth's goods	
	Roman		
(c	پاکِستانی لوگ Pakistani people	پاکستانی کھانا Pakistani food	
	Roman		
(d	کُچھ لوگ some people	کچھ کتابیں some books	کچھ پنجُابی لوگ some Punjabi people
	Roman		
(e	پنجابی نوجوان Punjabi youth	پنجاب کا بُینک Punjab's bank	بینک کا کام bank('s) work
	Roman		

(f	ہسپُتال کا کام hospital('s) work	ہسپتال کا نام the name of the hospital	کتاب کا نام the name of the book
Roman			
(g	بینک کا نام the name of the bank	کِتنا کام how much work?	کتنا پیسہ how much money?
Roman			
(h	بہُت پیسہ much money	بہت لوگ many people	بہت پاکستانی لوگ many Pakistani people
Roman			
(i	مُسلمان لوگ Muslim people	کچھ مسلمان some Muslims	مولُوی کا کام the maulvi's work
Roman			
(j	مولوی کا سامان the maulvi's goods	آپ کا بچُپن your childhood	بچپن کی بات a childhood('s) matter
Roman			

6. Read the following graffiti and translate it into English.

(a وہ بھی پاکستانی ہے۔

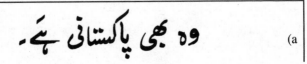

آپ بھی پاکستانی ہیں۔	(b
ہم سب پاکستانی ہیں۔	(c
ہم سب کا مُلک ہے پاکستان۔	(d

Glossary

he/she/it/that (pronounced irregularly as **vo**)	وہ
also	بھی
is	ہَے
you (polite)	آپ
are	ہَیں
we	ہم
all	سب
country (m)	مُلک

Summary

- و **vāo** represents three long vowel sounds and the semi-vowel **v**.
- At the beginning of a word, و **vāo** represents **v**.
- The three long vowels **ū**, **o**, and **au** are represented at the beginning of a word by ا **alif** and و **vāo**.
- When و **vāo** is followed by either ا **alif** or ی **ye** in the middle of a word, it often represents the semi-vowel **v**.
- The pronunciation of the pronoun وہ **vah** (**vo**) (he, she, it, that) is irregular.

Answers to practices

1. a) **jūblī** b) **jāsūs** c) **bīvī** d) **bojhal**
2. a) **cauk** b) **ū̃cā** c) **maut** d) **sautelā**
3. a) جوان b) چاول c) سموسا

   d) مَوسم e) سُوُکھنا f) کُیوں
4. a) م س ل م ا ن **muslamān**

   b) م و ل و ی **maulvī**

   c) پ ی ن س ل **pensil**

   d) ن و ج و ا ن **nau javān**

   e) ہ س پ ت ا ل **haspitāl**

5. a) **āp kī kitāb, lāl kitāb** b) **naujavān kī kitāb, naujavān kā sāmān** c) **pākistānī log, pākistānī khānā** d) **kuch log, kuch kitābẽ, kuch panjābī log** e) **panjābī naujavān, panjāb kā baink, baink kā kām** f) **haspatāl kā kām, haspatāl kā nām, kitāb kā nām** g) **baink kā nām, kitnā kām, kitnā paisah (paisā)** h) **bahut paisah (paisā), bahut log, bahut pākistānī log** i) **musalmān log, kuch musalmān, maulvī kā kām** j) **maulvī kā sāmān, āp kā bacpan, bacpan kī bāt**

6. a) **vah (vo) bhī pākistānī hai** he/she also is Pakistani b) **āp bhī pākistānī haĩ** You also are Pakistani c) **ham sab pākistānī haĩ** we are all Pakistani d) **ham sab kā mulk hai pākistān** Pakistan belongs to us all (we all's country is Pakistan)

7 UNIT 7

Five characters are introduced in this unit. This brings the total number of characters thus far to twenty. All five of these characters represent consonant sounds in Urdu. Three of these are connectors and two are non-connectors.

د	**dāl**	non-connector
ر	**re**	non-connector
ح	**baṛī he**	connector
ش	**shīn**	connector
ص	**svād**	connector

Pronunciation

For most Urdu speakers the pronunciation of the characters ح **baṛī he** and ص **svād** is almost exactly the same as that of ہ **choṭī he** and س **sīn**, introduced in earlier units. This is because the sounds that these characters represent in Arabic were gradually diluted in Urdu but the original spellings of words in which they occur have been maintained. For this reason, they are represented in Roman script in this book by the same letters (**h** and **s**). It is important to remember that the letter **h** is also used to represent the aspiration of a consonant.

Character	Name	Transliteration	Pronunciation
د	**dāl**	**d**	**d** in **d**one (the tip of the tongue touches the back of the top teeth)
ر	**re**	**r**	**r** in **r**un
ح	**baṛī he**	**h**	**h** in **h**ut
ش	**shīn**	**sh**	**sh** in **sh**un
ص	**svād**	**s**	**s** in **s**un

Positional forms

It is often difficult for the beginner to distinguish between the non-connecting characters د **dāl** and ر **re** because of their similar shape. It will help to remember that د **dāl** joins to the preceding character at the middle whereas ر **re** joins at the top. These characters are also often confused with the character و **vāo**.

Name	Final form (unjoined)	Final form (joined)	Medial form	Initial form	Transliteration
dāl	د	ـد	ـد	د	**d**
re	ر	ـر	ـر	ر	**r**
baṛī he	ح	ـح	ـحـ	حـ	**h**
shīn	ش	ـش	ـشـ	شـ	**sh**
svād	ص	ـص	ـصـ	صـ	**s**

Writing practice

Practise forming these characters according to the guidelines given.

د **dāl**

initial and final (unjoined) form

medial and final (joined) form

ر **re**

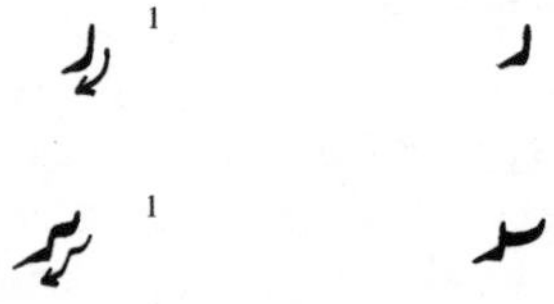

initial and final (unjoined) form

medial and final (joined) form

ح **baṛī he**

For a description of how to draw the forms of the character ح **baṛī he**, see the formation of ج **jīm** on p.17.

ش **shīn**

For a description of how to draw the forms of the character ش **shīn**, see the formation of س **sīn** on p.37.

ص **svād**

initial form

medial form

final form (joined)

final form (unjoined)

Reading and writing practice

1. Write the following words according to the guidelines given and then provide their Roman equivalents.

Meaning

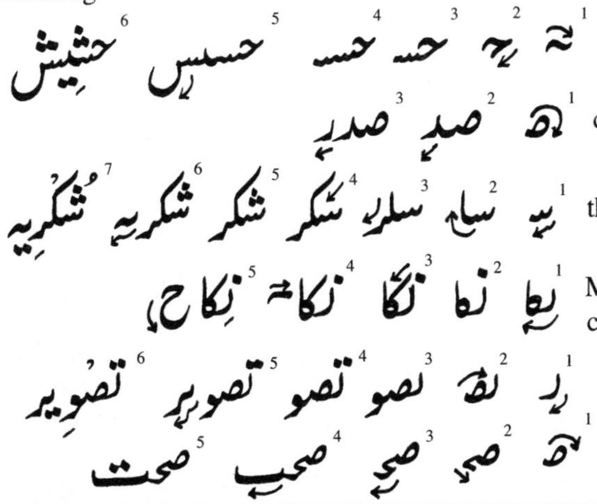

hashish (f) (a

chairman (m) (b

thank you (m) (c

Muslim wedding ceremony (m) (d

picture (f) (e

health (f) (f

2. Read the following words and write them in Roman script.

Meaning	Roman	Urdu
dhal (f)		دال (a
night (f)		رات (b
soap (m)		صابُن (c
ruler, governor (m)		حاکِم (d
splendour, lustre (f)		شان (e
washerman (m)		دھوبی (f
rail (f)		ریل (g

Meaning	Roman	Urdu
province (m)		صُوبہ (h
life, existence (f)		حیات (i
grandeur, dignity (f)		شَوکت (j

3. Join the appropriate forms of the characters supplied to form the following words.

	Roman	Meaning
= د + ا + ب + آ	ābād	populated (a
= م + ا + ر + آ	ārām	rest/respite (m) (b
= ی + م + د + آ	ādmī	man (m) (c
= ر + گ + ا	agar	if (d
= د + ح + ر + س	sarhad	border (f) (e
= و + د + ر + ا	urdū	Urdu (f) (f
= ش + ش + و + ک	koshish	effort/endeavour (f) (g

4. Read the following words quickly, focusing on the characters that are similar in shape, and then write them in Roman script.

روتا	دو	دارُو	دَرد	(a
to cry	two	medicine (f)	pain (m)	
دَور	دونوں	دُوسرا	اُردُو	(b
tour (m)	both	second/other	Urdu (f)	

(c	دُودھ	دھوبی	اِرادہ	بدْتر	
	milk (m)	washerman (m)	intention (m)	worse	
(d	شب	سب	شاہ	سانپ	
	night (f)	all	ruler (m)	snake (m)	
(e	دسْت	راسْتہ	دُشْمن	رِشْتہ	
	hand (m)	way/path (m)	enemy (m)	relation (m)	
(f	حج	حد	حرام	رُجْحان	حرْج
	pilgrimage (m)	extreme/limit (f)	forbidden	inclination (m)	damage/loss (m)

5. Read the following advertisement and translate it into English. A glossary of unfamiliar words can be found on page 62.

(a پنجاب نیشنل بینک

(b لاہور

(c آپ کا بینک

(d آپ کے ساتھ

(e آج بھی کل بھی

(f ہمیشہ

(g بھروسے کا نِشان

Glossary

Punjab	پنجاب
national	نیشنل
bank (m)	بینک
Lahore	لاہور
you	آپ
with	کے ساتھ
today	آج
tomorrow	کل
forever	ہمیشہ
reliance/trust (m)	بھروسا
sign (m)	نِشان
even/also	بھی

Summary

- The tip of the tongue touches the top of the back teeth in the pronunciation of د **dāl**.
- The characters ہ **choṭī he** and ح **baṛī he** represent the same sound for most speakers and are both represented in Roman script by the letter **h** in this book.
- س **sīn** and ص **svād** also represent the same sound and are both represented by **s** in Roman script in this book.
- د **dāl** and ر **re** are most easily distinguished by focusing on the point at which the preceding character joins them.

- ش **shīn** has the same basic shape as س **sīn**.
- The shape of ح **baṛī he** is the same as that of ج **jīm**. Therefore, they are grouped together in the alphabet.

Answers to practices

1. a) **hashīsh** b) **sadar** c) **shukriyah (shukriyā)** d) **nikāh** e) **tasvīr** f) **sahat (sehat)**

2. a) **dāl** b) **rāt** c) **sābun** d) **hākim** e) **shān** f) **dhobī** g) **rel** h) **sūbah (sūbā)** i) **hayāt** j) **shaukat**

3. a) آباد b) آرام c) آدمی d) اگر e) سرحد f) اُردو g) کوشش

4 a) **dard, dārū, do, ronā** b) **urdū, dūsra, donõ, daurah (daurā)** c) **dūdh, dhobī, irādah (irādā), badtar** d) **shab, sab, shāh, sā̃p** e) **dast, rāstah (rāsta), dushman, rishtah (rishtā)** f) **haj, had, harām, rujhān, harj**

5. a) **panjāb neshanal baink** Punjab National Bank b) **lahaur** Lahore c) **āp kā baink** your bank d) **āp ke sāth** with you e) **āj bhī kal bhī** today also tomorrow also f) **hameshah (hameshā)** forever g) **bharose kā nishān** the sign of reliance

UNIT 8

The five characters introduced in this unit occur mainly in words that have come into Urdu from Persian, Arabic and English. Three are connectors and two are non-connectors. They are:

خ	**khe**	connector
ذ	**zāl**	non-connector
ز	**ze**	non-connector
ض	**zād**	connector
ف	**fe**	connector

Pronunciation

Three of these five characters represent the same sound for most speakers of Urdu. As with the characters ح **baṛī he** and ص **svād** in Unit 7, the reason for this is that the Arabic phonetic values of the characters have been lost in Urdu but the original spellings of the words in which they occur have been retained.

Character	Name	Transliteration	Pronunciation
خ	**khe**	**kh**	similar to **ch** in the Scottish word lo**ch**
ذ	**zāl**		
ز	**ze**	**z**	z in **z**ebra
ض	**zād**		
ف	**fe**	**f**	f in **f**un

Positional forms

The basic shape of the character خ **khe** is the same as that of ج **jīm** and with the introduction of خ **khe** this series of characters is now complete (ج **jīm**, چ **cīm**, ح **baṛī he**, and خ **khe**). The basic shapes of the characters ذ **zāl** and ز **ze** are the same as those of د **dāl** and ر **re**. For this reason they too belong to the same series. ض **zvād** is identical in shape to ص **svād**. Finally the linear portion of the character ف **fe** is also similar to the basic shape of the **be** series of characters although it is not included with them in that series. The line under the Roman representation of the character خ **khe** is used to distinguish it from the aspirated form of the character ک **kāf** (کھ **kh**).

Name	Final form (unjoined)	Final form (joined)	Medial form	Initial form	Transliteration
khe	خ	ـخ	ـخـ	خـ	**kh**
zāl	ذ	ـذ	ـذ	ذ	**z**
ze	ز	ـز	ـز	ز	**z**
zād	ض	ـض	ـضـ	ضـ	**z**
fe	ف	ـف	ـفـ	فـ	**f**

Writing practice

Practise writing the various forms of these characters.

خ **khe**

For a description of how to draw the forms of the character خ **khe**, see the formation of ج **jīm** on p.17.

ذ **zāl**

For a description of how to draw the forms of the character ذ **zāl**, see the formation of د **dāl** on p.58.

ز **ze**

For a description of how to draw the forms of the character ز **ze**, see the formation of ر **re** on p.58.

ض **zād**

For a description of how to draw the forms of the character ض **zād**, see the formation of ص **svād** on p.58.

ف **fe**

initial form

medial form

final form (joined)

final form (unjoined)

Reading and writing practice

1. Following the guidelines given, write these words in Urdu and then provide their Roman equivalents.

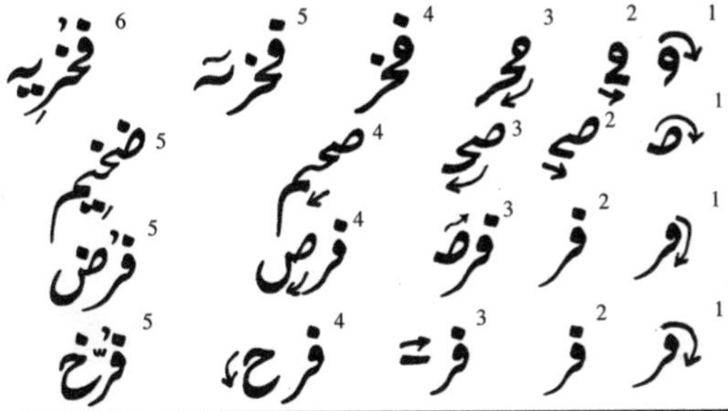

Meaning
ostentation (m) (a
fat (b
duty (m) (c
beautiful (also a name) (d

2. Read the following words and write them in Roman script.

Meaning	Roman	Urdu
special		خاص (a
fever (m)		بُخار (b
direction (m)		رُخ (c
a little		ذرا (d
religion (m)		مذہب (e
tasty		لذیذ (f
a cold (m)		زُکام (g
elderly		بُزُرگ (h
thing (f)		چیز (i

Meaning	Roman	Urdu	
certainly		ضُرور	(j
Sir!		حُضُور	(k
a (water) tank (n)		حَوض	(l
worry (f)		فِکر	(m
journey (m)		سفر	(n
clean		صاف	(o

3. Join the appropriate forms of the characters supplied to write the following words.

	Roman	Meaning
= ر + ب + خ	**khabar**	news (f) (a
= ت + خ + ت	**takht**	board, seat (m) (b
= خ + س + ن	**naskh**	Arabic script (m) (c
= ن + ہ + ذ	**zahan (zehn)**	mind (m) (d
= ہ + ب + ذ + ج	**jazbah (jazbā)**	emotion (m) (e
= ن + ا + ب + ز	**zabān**	tongue/language (f) (f
= ی + گ + د + ن + ز	**zindagī**	life (f) (g
= ر + ا + ز + ا + ب	**bāzār**	market (m) (h
= ی + ز + ب + س	**sabzī**	vegetable (f) (i
= ل + ض + ف	**fazl**	grace, mercy, (m) (j
= ہ + ت + ف + ہ	**haftah (haftā)**	week (m) (k
= د + ی + ف + س	**safed**	white (l

4. Read the following groups of words, focusing on those characters that look similar in form, then write them in Roman script.

درزی	درْوازه	روز	زرْد	(a
tailor (m)	door (m)	daily	pale	
ذِمہ دار	راز	دُکان دار	مزہ دار	(b
responsible	secret (m)	shopkeeper (m)	enjoyable	
خبر	حل	چُست	جلن	(c
news (f)	solution (m)	agile	envy (f)	
سجانا	صاحب	بخْش	لالچی	(d
to decorate	sahib (m)	giving/granting	greedy	

5. Read the titles of the following films showing at the Jubilee Cinema. Write them in Roman script and then translate them into English.

(a) جُوبلی سِینما کراچی

(b) روزانہ چار شو
بارہ تِین چھ نَو بجے

(c) آخِری سفر

(d) زِندگی اَور مَوت

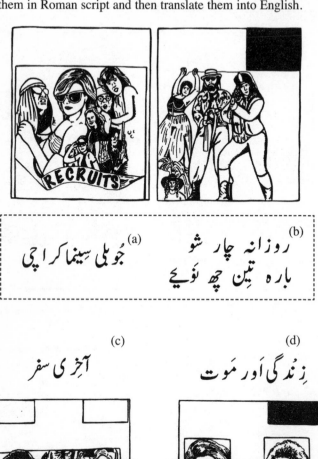

(e)

خبُردار!

(f)

بے انُصافی

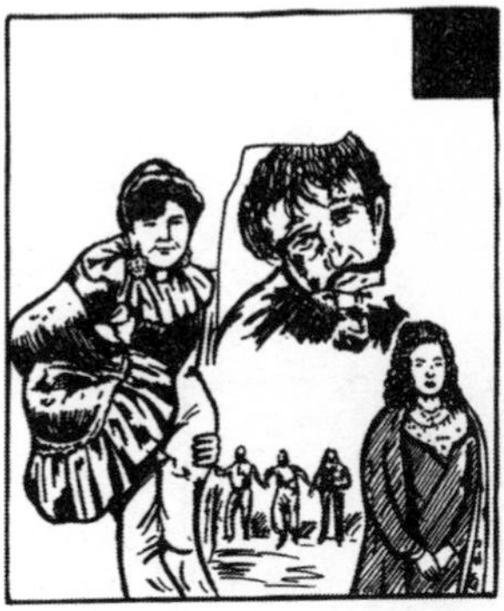

(g)

منُزِل ابھی دُور ہے

(h)

جُرم اَور سزا

Glossary

The following words appear in the film titles.

jubilee	جُوبْلی
cinema (m)	سِنیما
four	چار
daily	روزانہ
shows (m)	شو
twelve	بارہ
three	تِین
six	چھ
nine	نَو
o'clock	بجے
final	آخْری
journey	سفر
and	اَور
beware!	خبرْدار
destination (f)	منْزِل

still	ابھی
far	دُور
is	ہَے
injustice (f)	بے اِنصافی
crime (m)	جُرم
punishment (f)	سزا
life (f)	زِندگی
death (f)	مَوت

Summary

- The characters ذ **zāl**, ز **ze**, and ض **zād** all represent the same sound (**z**) for most Urdu speakers.
- The character خ **<u>kh</u>e** completes the series of four characters that have an identical shape to that of ج **jīm** (ج **jīm**, چ **cīm**, ح **baṛī he**, خ **<u>kh</u>e**).
- ذ **zāl** and ز **ze** have the same basic shape as د **dāl** and ر **re**.
- The basic shape of ف **fe** is the same as that of ب **be**.

Answers to practices

1. a) **fa<u>kh</u>riyah (fakhriyā)** b) **za<u>kh</u>īm** c) **farz** d) **farru<u>kh</u>**

2. a) **<u>kh</u>ās** b) **bu<u>kh</u>ār** c) **ru<u>kh</u>** d) **zarā** e) **mazhab** f) **lazīz** g) **zukām** h) **buzurg** i) **cīz** j) **zarūr** k) **huzūr** l) **hauz** m) **fikr** n) **safar** o) **sāf**

3. a) خَبر b) تخت c) نسخ d) ذہن e) جذبہ f) زبان g) زندگی

h) بازار i) سنبری j) فضل k) ہفتہ l) سفید

4. a) zard, roz, darvāzah (darvāzā), darzī b) mazahdār (mazedār), dukāndār, rāz, zimmahdār (zimmedār) c) jalan, cust, hal, <u>kh</u>abar d) lālcī, ba<u>kh</u>sh, sāhab, sajānā

5. a) jūblī sinemā karācī Jubilee Cinema Karachi b) rozānah (rozānā) cār sho, bārah, tīn, cha (chai), nau baje four shows daily, twelve, three, six, nine o'clock c) ā<u>kh</u>irī safar, 'The Final Journey' d) zindagī aur maut, 'Life and Death' e) <u>kh</u>abardār!, 'Beware!' f) beinsāfī, 'Injustice' g) manzil abhī dūr hai, 'The Destination is Still Far' h) jurm aur sazah (sazā), 'Crime and Punishment'

9 UNIT 9

In this unit three connectors and two non-connectors are introduced. The first three characters were added to the alphabet to represent sounds that occur in Urdu but not in Arabic or Persian.

ٹ	**ṭe**	connector
ڈ	**ḍāl**	non-connector
ڑ	**ṛe**	non-connector
غ	**g͟hain**	connector
ق	**qāf**	connector

Pronunciation

The first three characters represent the retroflex sounds in Urdu. A dot is placed under the letter in the Roman script to distinguish these characters from the dental sounds ت **te** and د **dāl**, and the voiced alveolar ر **re**, introduced in Units 5 and 7. The retroflex sounds are produced by placing the tip of the tongue on the roof of the mouth while the dental sounds are produced by placing the tip of the tongue up against the back of the top teeth. The final two characters in this unit, غ **g͟hain** and ق **qāf**, occur in words that have come into Urdu from Arabic and Persian.

Character	Name	Transliteration	Pronunciation
ٹ	**ṭe**	**ṭ**	the underside of the tip of the tongue touches the roof of the mouth
ڈ	**ḍāl**	**ḍ**	as above but this sound is voiced
ڑ	**ṛe**	**ṛ**	the underside of the tip of the tongue touches the roof of the mouth and, without resting there, is flapped downwards
غ	**<u>gh</u>ain**	**<u>gh</u>**	voiced velar or post-velar fricative, similar to the sound made when gargling; this is the voiced counterpart of خ **<u>kh</u>e**
ق	**qāf**	**q**	a **k** sound made as far back in the throat as possible

Positional forms

The basic shape of ٹ **ṭe** is the same as that of ب **be**, پ **pe** and ت **te**. There is only one more character (introduced in Unit 10) to complete this, the second series. ڈ **ḍāl** and ڑ **ṛe** are part of the same series as د **dāl**, ذ **zāl**, ر **re** and ز **ze**. On account of its shape, the character ق **qāf** is conventionally grouped together with the character ف **fe** although the loop is the same shape as that of ن **nūn**, whereas the bottom of ف **fe** is the same as the linear portion of the characters in the ب **be** series.

Name	Final form (unjoined)	Final form (joined)	Medial form	Initial form	Transliteration
ṭe	ٹ	ـٹ	ـٹـ	ٹـ	**ṭ**
ḍāl	ڈ	ـڈ	ـڈ	ڈ	**ḍ**
ṛe	ڑ	ـڑ	ـڑ	ڑ	**ṛ***
ghain	غ	ـغ	ـغـ	غـ	**gh**
qāf	ق	ـق	ـقـ	قـ	**q**

*The character ڑ **ṛe** never occurs at the beginning of a word but this initial form does appear after a non-connector.

Writing practice

Practise drawing the various forms of the characters according to the guidelines given.

ٹ **ṭe**

For a description of how to draw the four basic shapes of ٹ **ṭe**, see the formation of ب **be** on p.2.

ڈ **ḍāl**

For a description of how to draw the four basic shapes of ڈ **ḍāl**, see the formation of د **dāl** on p.58.

ڑ **ṛe**

For a description of how to draw the four basic shapes of ڑ **ṛe**, see the formation of ر **re** on p.58.

غ **ghain**

initial form

medial form

final form (joined)

final form (unjoined)

ق qāf

initial form

medial form

final form (joined)

final form (unjoined)

Reading and writing practice

1. Practise forming the following words according to the directions and then write the Roman equivalents.

Meaning

cold (f) (a

rights (m) (b

light (m) (c

slander (f) (d

Meaning

قَدِیم ⁶ قَدِیمؔ ⁵ قَدِیؔ ⁴ قَد ³ مِد ² (وَ ¹   ancient (e

غَوؔر ⁴ غْو ³ عو ² عؔ ¹   deep thought (m) (f

2. Read the following words in Urdu and transliterate them into Roman script.

Meaning	Roman	Urdu
post (f)		ڈاک (a
stamp/ticket (m)		ٹِکٹ (b
doctor (m)		ڈاکٹر (c
to read/study		پڑھنا (d
mountain (m)		پہاڑ (e
slave (m)		غُلام (f
Mughal		مُغل (g
chicken (m)		مُرغ (h
able/capable		قابِل (i
time (m)		وقت (j
difference (m)		فرُق (k

3. Using the appropriate forms of the characters given write the following words.

	Roman	Meaning
ڈ + ی + ڑ + ھ =	**ḍeṛh**	1 1/2 (a
ح + ق + ی + ق + ت =	**haqīqat**	reality (f) (b
ل + ڑ + ک + ا =	**laṛkā**	boy (m) (c
د + ا + ر + و + غ + ہ =	**dāroghah (dāroghā)**	police inspector (m) (d
ی + و + ن + ی + و + ر + س + ٹ + ی =	**yūnīvarsiṭī**	university (f) (e

4. Read the following phrases, paying close attention to the pronunciation of words that are repeated but for which vowel-markers are provided only the first time the word appears. Note that the order of the words in Urdu is, in most cases, exactly the same as in English, except that they run from right to left.

(a ایک چھوٹی لڑکی

A (one) small girl

(b دو ذہِین لڑکیاں

two intelligent girls

(c تِین لڑکوں کے نام

the names of three boys

(d چار قَومی زبانیں

four national languages

(e پانچ قومی اخباروں میَں

in five national newspapers

(f اُردُو زبان

Urdu language

(g اردو کا اخبار

Urdu('s) newspaper

(h چھ مُقامی زبانیں

six local languages

(i سات مقامی لوگوں کے نام

seven local people's names

(j دھوبی کا مکان

the washerman's house

(k پھُولوں کا رنگ

the colour of the flowers

(l آٹھ پھولوں کی قِیمت

the price of eight flowers

(m نَو ہفُتوں کا وُقت

nine weeks' time

(n ٹھنُڈ کا مَوسم

the cold('s) weather

5. Read the following advertisement and determine what is being sold. Write out the advertisement in Roman script.

(a اِشتُہار

(b سَیل سَیل سَیل

(c پُرانی گاڑِیاں

(d	اچّھی کُوالِٹی بُہت کم قِیمت میَں
(e	مزُدا سُوزُوکی نِسان ٹویوٹا
(f	دیر مت کرو

Glossary

advertisement (m)	اِشتہار
sale (m)	سیَل
old	پُرانی
cars (f)	گاڑِیاں
good	اچّھی
quality (f)	کُوالِٹی
very	بُہت
less	کم
price (f)	قِیمت
in	میَں
delay	دیر
not	مت
do	کرو

6. Look up the following timetable and find out where the following airline flies in the subcontinent.

سہارا اِنٹر نیشنل (a

وقت	روز	منزِل	روانگی	(b
صُبح آٹھ بجے	منگل	کابُل	دہلی	(c
شام سات بجے	روز	کلکتہ	لاہور	(d
شام پانچ بجے	پِیر	کراچی	کاٹھمانڈُو	(e
صُبح دس بجے	بُدھ	ڈھاکہ	اِسلام آباد	(f

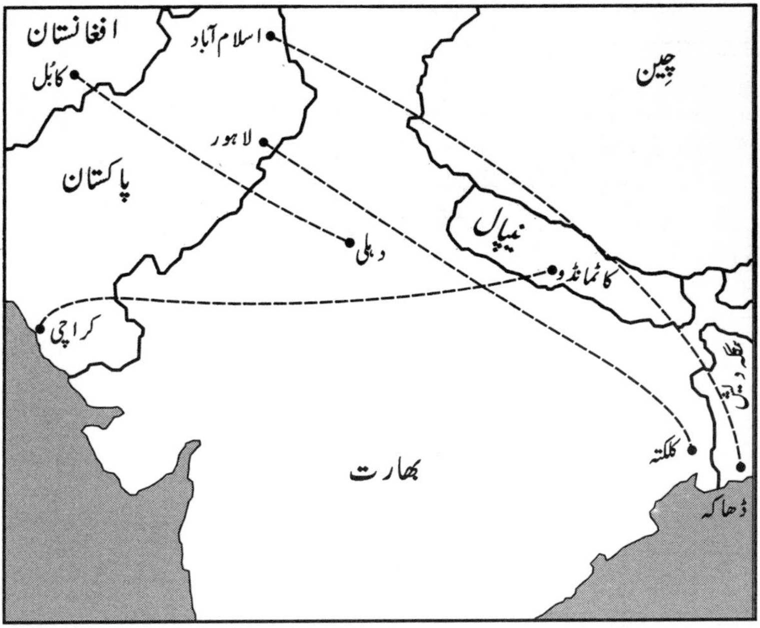

Glossary

help/support (m)	سہارا
international	اِنٹرنیشنل
departure (f)	روانگی
destination (f)	منزِل
day (m)	روز
time (m)	وقت
Tuesday (m)	منگل
Monday (m)	پیر
Wednesday (m)	بُدھ
daily	روز
morning (f)	صُبح
evening (f)	شام
eight	آٹھ
seven	سات
five	پانچ
ten	دس
o'clock	بجے

Summary

- ٹ **ṭe**, ڈ **ḍāl** and ڑ **ṛe** are retroflex sounds in Urdu. Retroflex sounds are produced by placing the tip of the tongue on the roof of the mouth and, in the case of ڑ **ṛe**, flapping it down as the air escapes.
- غ **ghain** and ق **qāf** occur in words that have come into Urdu from Arabic and Persian.
- The sound غ **ghain** represents is close to that made when gargling.
- ق **qāf** is similar to the sound **k** but produced as far back in the mouth as possible.

Answers to practices

1. a) **ṭhanḍ** b) **huqūq** c) **cirāgh** d) **cughlī** e) **qadīm** f) **ghaur**

2. a) **ḍāk** b) **ṭikaṭ** c) **ḍākṭar** d) **paṛhnā** e) **pahāṛ** f) **ghulām** g) **mughal** h) **murgh** i) **qābil** j) **vaqt** k) **farq**

3. a) ڈیڑھ b) حقیقت c) لڑکا d) داروغہ

e) یُونِیوَرسِٹی

4. a) **ek choṭī laṛkī** b) **do zahīn laṛkyā̃** c) **tīn laṛkõ ke nām** d) **cār qaumī zabānẽ** e) **pā̃c qaumī akhbārõ mẽ** f) **urdū zabān** g) **urdū kā akhbār** h) **cha (che) muqāmī zabānẽ** i) **sāt muqāmī logõ ke nām** j) **dhobī kā makān** k) **phūlõ kā rang** l) **āṭh phūlõ kī qīmat** m) **nau haftõ kā vaqt** n) **ṭhanḍ kā mausam**

5. a) **ishtahār** advertisement b) **sail** sale c) **purānī gāṛiyā̃** old cars d) **acchī kvāliṭī** good quality, **bahut kam qīmat mẽ** for (in) a low price e) **mazdā, sūzūkī, nisān, ṭoyoṭā** f) **der mat karo** don't delay

6. a) **sahārā inṭarneshanal** Sahara International b) **ravāngī manzil roz vaqt** departure destination day time c) **dahlī kābul mangal subah āṭh baje** Delhi Kabul Tuesday morning eight o'clock d) **lāhaur kalkattah (kalkattā) roz shām sāt baje** Lahore Calcutta daily evening seven o'clock e) **kāṭhmānḍū karācī pīr shām pā̃c baje** Kathmandu Karachi Monday evening five o'clock f) **islāmābād ḍhākah (ḍhākā) budh subah das baje** Islamabad Dhaka Wednesday morning ten o'clock

10 UNIT 10

In this unit the final five characters are introduced. They occur in words that have come into Urdu from Arabic and Persian. Four of them are connectors. The first two characters occur rarely in Urdu.

ث	**se**	connector
ژ	**zhe**	non-connector
ط	**to'e**	connector
ظ	**zo'e**	connector
ع	**'ain**	connector

Pronunciation

The first four characters represent more or less sounds that are also represented by characters introduced in earlier units. The final character, ع **'ain**, however, may represent several sounds and is even silent in certain words.

Character	Name	Transliteration	Pronunciation
ث	**se**	**s**	s in **s**in
ژ	**zhe**	**z**	z in plea**s**ure
ط	**to'e**	**t**	t in **t**on
ظ	**zo'e**	**z**	z in **z**ip
ع	**'ain**	**'**	see later in unit

The characters that represent one and the same sound for Urdu speakers are:

ذ **zāl**	ز **ze**	ض **zād**	ظ **zo'e**	all represent the sound **z**
ث **se**	س **sīn**	ص **svād**		all represent the sound **s**
ت **te**	and	ط **to'e**		represent the dental sound **t**
ہ **choṭī he**	and	ح **baṛī he**		both represent the sound **h** for most speakers in most contexts

Positional forms

Most of the characters introduced here have identical shapes to those of characters that were introduced in earlier units. With the introduction of the character ث **se**, the ب **be** series of characters is also now complete (ب **be**, پ **pe**, ت **te**, ٹ **ṭe**, ث **se**). ژ **zhe** has the same shape as ر **re**, ز **ze** and ڑ **ṛe**. Finally, the basic shape of ط **to'e** and ظ **zo'e** is the same. As a result, all of these characters are classed together in the alphabet.

Name	Final form (unjoined)	Final form (joined)	Medial form	Initial form	Transliteration
se	ث	ـث	ـثـ	ثـ	**s**
zhe	ژ	ـژ	ـژ	ژ	**z**
to'e	ط	ـط	ـطـ	طـ	**t**
zo'e	ظ	ـظ	ـظـ	ظـ	**z**
'ain	ع	ـع	ـعـ	عـ	**'**

Writing practice

Practise forming these characters according to the guidelines given.

ث **se**

For a description of how to draw the four shapes of ث **se**, see the formation of ب **be** on p.2.

ژ **zhe**

For a description of how to draw the four shapes of ژ **zhe**, see the formation of ر **re** on p.58.

ط **to'e**

ط initial form

ط medial form

ط final form (joined)

ط final form (unjoined)

ظ **zo'e**

For a description of how to draw the four shapes of ظ **zo'e**, see the formation of ط **to'e** just given.

ع **'ain**

For a description of how to draw the four shapes of ع **'ain**, see the formation of غ **ghain** on p.78.

Pronunciation of ع **'ain**

ع **'ain** is a glottal fricative in Arabic but has all but lost this value in Urdu. (A glottal fricative is the sound made when the throat muscles are highly constricted and the vocal chords vibrate. It is similar to the sound made when retching.) In Urdu ع **'ain** either has little or no pronunciation or produces an effect on a preceding or following vowel. The following examples are provided to indicate possible effects ع **'ain** can have on the pronunciation of vowels in particular words.

ع 'ain representing a vowel

In many words, ع **'ain** has no real pronunciation of its own but simply indicates the presence of a vowel.

عدالت	عِمارت	عُمر	عیسا
'adālat	**'imārat**	**'umr**	**'īsā**
law court (f)	building (f)	age (f)	Jesus
عَیش	عَورت	عام	دُعا
'aish	**'aurat**	**'ām**	**du'ā**
luxury (m)	woman (f)	ordinary	prayer (f)

ع 'ain influencing the pronunciation of a vowel

In the middle of a word, ع **'ain** may influence a preceding short vowel. This may have the effect of lengthening it. In the following words the Roman transliteration is given first representing the spelling of the word. This is followed in parentheses by the pronunciation.

استعمال	شعر	معلوم
isti'māl	**shĕ'r***	**ma'lūm**
(istemāl)	**(sher)**	**(mālūm)**
use (m)	a couplet (poetry) (m)	known
جعلی	شعلہ	اعتبار
ja'lī	**shŏ'lah***	**i'tibār**
(jālī)	**(sholā)**	**(etibār)**
forged	flame (m)	faith (m)

*The symbols above these vowels indicate that they are shorter than the vowels **e** and **o**.

جمع	مواقع	توقع
jama'	**mavāqĕ'**	**tavvaqŏ'**
(jamā)	**(mavāqe)**	**(tavvaqo)**
collected	opportunities (m)	hope/expectation (f)

Silent ع 'ain

In some words ع **'ain** is not pronounced. This is often the case when it occurs at the end of a word and follows a long vowel.

مطبوع
matbū'
(matbū)
agreeable/laudable

ع ‘ain as a glottal stop

Occasionally ع **‘ain** may be pronounced as a glottal stop between two vowels. A glottal stop is the sound that is produced with the release of the glottis (the opening between the vocal cords). This is often lost in Urdu as indicated by the pronunciation in parentheses.

معاف	سعادت
mu‘āf	**sa‘ādat**
(māf)	**(sādat)**
forgiven	fortunate

Reading and writing practice

1. Practise forming the following words according to the guidelines given.

	Roman	Meaning
	**tabiya‘t** (**tabiyat**)	health, disposition (f) (a
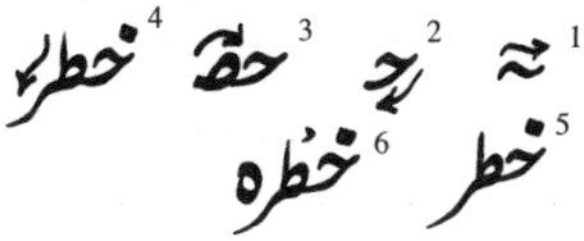	**<u>kh</u>atrah** (**<u>kh</u>atrā**)	danger (m) (b
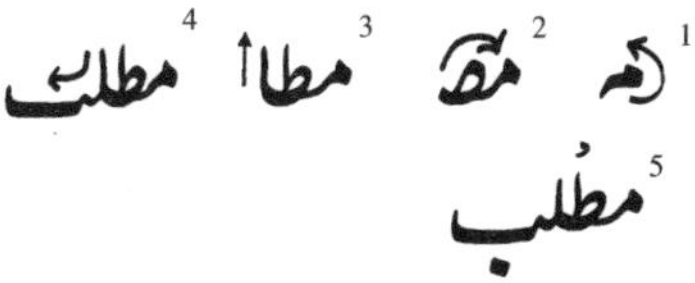	**matlab**	meaning (m) (c
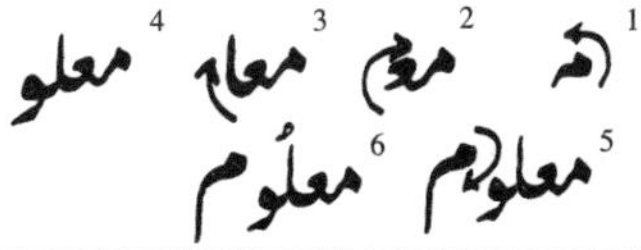	**ma‘lūm** (**mālūm**)	known (d

2. Read the following words and transliterate them into Roman script.

Meaning	Roman	Urdu
capacity (f)		حَیْثِیَت (a
debate, argument (f)		بَحْث (b
letters (m)		خُطُوط (c
surface (f)		سَطْح (d
apparent		ظاہِر (e
victorious		مُظَّفَر (f

3. Join the appropriate forms of the following characters and write the words listed.

	Roman	Meaning
ق + ط + ع + ی =	qata'ia	absolutely (a
ا + ع + ظ + م =	a'zam (āzam)	greatest (b
و + ظ + ی + ف + ہ =	vazīfah (vazīfā)	stipend (m) (c

4. Complete the following words by writing in the appropriate number of dots or the symbol that resembles a flat sign above and below characters.

	Roman	Meaning
حصص	tahqīq (tehqīq)	inquiry (f) (a
سحدہ	sanjīdah (sanjīdā)	serious (b
ماحوس	nā<u>kh</u>ush*	unhappy (c

	Roman	Meaning
رىفرىحرىس	**refrījareshan**	refrigeration (m) (d
دىىل ىكىمس	**ḍenṭal ṭeknishan**	dental technician (m) (e
حفاظت	**hifāzat**	protection (f) (f
ىحىں	**pacpan**	fifty-five (g

*The pronunciation of this word is exceptional. The character و **vāo** is written but not really pronounced.

5. Look at the restaurant bill and try to determine what the customers on table four had for dinner. Transliterate these dishes into Roman script.

(a محفل ریستوران لاہور

(b دو روغن جوش ....

(c ایک چکن قورمہ ....

(d تین پالک پنیر ....

(e پانچ نان ....

(f چار روٹی ....

(g چاول ....

(h دال ....

(i چھ گلاب جامن ....

Glossary

two	دو
three	تِین
four	چار
five	پانچ
six	چھ
rice	چاول
bread	نان
roti	روٹی
daal	دال

6. What do the following newspaper headlines say? Read them through and then transliterate them into Roman script.

(a روزنامہ جنگ

(b ٹِیم کی بَیٹِنگ کی فِکر نہِیں وسِیم اکرم

(c لاہَور کے عَوامی ہسپتال مَیں آج ہڑُتال

(d غرِیبی ہٹانے کی مُہِم کا اعلان

Glossary

daily	روزُنامہ
war	جُنگ
team's	ٹیم کی
batting's	بیٹِنگ کی
worry	فِکُر
no	نِہیں
general	عَوامی
in hospital (m)	ہُسپتال میَں
today	آج
strike	ہُڑتال
poverty	غرِیبی
removing's	ہٹانے کی
campaign's (f)	مُہِم
call (m)	اعلان

The small symbol that appears in caption (b) is used to denote a name.

NB

کا **kā**, کے **ke**, کی **kī** = 's

Summary

- The character ث **se** completes the ب **be** series (ب **be**, پ **pe**, ت te, ٹ **ṭe**, ث **se**).
- ژ **zhe** is grouped with the ر **re** series of characters (ر **re**, ز **ze**, ڑ **ṛe**, ژ **zhe**).
- The character ع **'ain** either represents a short vowel, is not pronounced or may influence the pronunciation of vowels in a word.

Answers to practices

2. a) **haisīyat** b) **bahas** (**behas**) c) **khutūt** d) **satah** (**sateh**) e) **zāhir** f) **muzaffar**

3. a) قطعی b) اعظم c) وظیفہ

4. a) تحقیق b) سنجیدہ c) ناخوش d) ریفریجریشن

e) ڈینٹل ٹیکنیشن f) حفاظت g) چکن

5. a) **mahfil** (**mehfil**) **restorān lāhaur**, Mehfil Restaurant, Lahore b) **do roghan josh**, two rogan josh c) **ek cikan qormah** (**qormā**), one chicken korma d) **tīn pālak panīr**, three spinach and cheese dishes e) **pā̃c nān**, five naan f) **cār roṭī**, four rotis g) **cāval**, rice h) **dāl**, daal i) **ch** (**che**) **gulāb jāmun**, six gulab jamun

6. a) **roznāmah** (**roznāmā**) **jang**, the daily war b) **ṭīm kī baiṭing kī fikr nahī̃ - wasīm akram**, the teams batting (is) not a worry - Wasim Akram c) **lāhaur ke 'avāmī haspatāl mẽ āj haṛtāl**, a strike in the Lahore('s) general hospital today d) **gharībī haṭāne kī muhim kā a'lān** (**elān**), poverty removing's campaign's announcement (announcement of a campaign to remove poverty)

11 UNIT 11

In this unit the symbol ء **hamzā** is introduced as well as exceptional forms of particular characters, the **izāfat** construction, the shortened ا **alif** and the doubling of short vowel-markers. Also included are some notes on exceptional pronunciations.

ء hamzā

ء **hamzā** performs several functions in Urdu, the most important of which is to indicate that one syllable in a word ends in a vowel and the next syllable begins with one. The shape of ء **hamzā** is identical to the top portion of the character ع **'ain** although it also appears in a form which is similar to the Roman letter **s**.

ء ٕ
hamzā

If the second syllable begins with a vowel represented by و **vāo**, the ء **hamzā** rests above the و **vāo**.

For example:

جاؤ	آؤں	چھوؤ
jāo	**āū̃**	**chūo**
go (imperative)	shall I come?	touch (imperative)

If the second syllable begins with a vowel represented by ی **ye**, ء **hamzā** is said to need a support on which to rest. This support may take several forms depending on the characters that surround ء **hamzā**.

For example:

ئ	ئے	ئی
بھائی	گئے	گئی
bhāī	**gae**	**gaī**
brother (m)	went (m pl.)	went (f sing.)

There are alternative spellings of some words in which ء **hamzā** occurs. In particular, verbs that end in a consonant to which the ending ئے **ie** is attached may be encountered with three different spellings.

For example:

چاہئے	چاہیے	چاہیئے
cāhie	**cāhie**	**cāhie**
	want/need	

ء **hamzā** is also used to mark the occurrence of two vowels one after the other in a word where the second vowel is not represented by ی **ye** or و **vāo**.

لائق
lāiq
worthy, capable

izāfat

izāfat is the name given to a short **e** vowel (pronounced as in the English word **bet**) that is used to mark a relationship between two words. It may be translated into the English **of** as in the phrase, '**the lion of Punjab**'. **izāfat** is represented in the Roman script in this book by the letter **e**. In Urdu it is represented in more than one way.

izāfat represented by ◌ِ zer

In most cases **izāfat** is represented by the vowel symbol ◌ِ **zer**. It is written under the final character of the first word in the phrase.

شیرِ پنجاب
sher -e-panjāb
the lion of Punjab

In many common compounds, ◌ِ **zer** indicating **izāfat** is not written but is pronounced.

For example:

طالبِ علم or طالب علم
tālib-e-'ilm
seeker of knowledge (a student) (m)

izāfat represented by ◌ٔ hamzā

The symbol ◌ٔ **hamzā** is used to represent **izāfat** when the first word ends in either ہ **choṭī he** or ی **ye**.

قطرۂ آب	ولئِ کامِل
qatrah-e-āb **(qatrā-e-āb)**	**valī-e-kāmil**
(a) drop of water (m)	perfect saint (m)

When **izāfat** follows a long **ā** vowel, it is written as ے **e**, with or without ء **hamzā** on top.

رُوئے زمِین	صدائے بلند
rū-e-zamīn	**sadā-e-buland**
the surface of the ground (f)	a high voice (f)

Modified forms of characters

Several characters in the Urdu alphabet may show slightly modified forms, some of which only do so when they precede or follow particular characters. Two of these, the modified forms of ک **kāf** and گ **gāf** followed by ا **alif** or ل **lām** were introduced in earlier units. Several more are examined now.

س sīn and ش shīn

The modified form of these characters occurs frequently in Urdu texts. In this form, the initial indented part of the character is replaced by a long sweeping stroke. This alternative form is found both in texts prepared by calligraphers and in ordinary handwritten Urdu. It is found particularly where two of these characters occur consecutively in a word.

پاکِستان	سستا	کوشِش
pakistān	**sastā**	**koshish**
Pakistan (m)	cheap	endeavour/try (f)

The indented portion of these characters is also abbreviated in some people's handwriting.

پسند
pasand
liked/chosen

The sweeping strokes of characters such as those in the ب **be** series and ک **kāf** and گ **gāf** are also occasionally extended in the final form according to the space on the page.

Modified characters in the ب be series

Characters in this series (including ی **ye** and ن **nūn**) show a slightly modified form when they occur initially or medially and precede characters in the ج **jīm** series, م **mīm** and ہ **choṭī he**.

نو	but	نہیں	بدتر	but	بچانا	تالی	but	تمہارا
nau		**nahī̃**	**badtar**		**bacānā**	**tālī**		**tumhārā**
nine		no	worse		to save	clapping		your
ہندو	but	پنجرا	لینا	but	پیچھے			
hindū		**pinjarā**	**lenā**		**pīche**			
Hindu		cage (m)	to take		behind			

The same characters are lengthened when they occur in the beginning of a word and are followed by either a character with a rounded form or س **sīn** or ش **shīn**.

پسند	تقاضا	بعد	نِکلنا
pasand	**taqāẓā**	**ba'd (bād)**	**nikalnā**
chosen	demand (m)	after	to emerge

ھ **do cashmī he** is occasionally found after ل **lām**, م **mīm** and ن **nūn** where ہ **choṭī he** would be expected.

تُمھارا	ھے
tumhārā	**hai**
your	is/are

Shortened ا alif

In a few Arabic words a short, detached form of ا **alif** occurs over the final form of ی **ye**. This is pronounced as a long **ā** vowel.

اعلیٰ	دعویٰ
a'lā	**da'vā**
(ālā)	**(dāvā)**
paramount, highest	law suit, claim (m)

Doubled vowel-markers

At the end of particular adverbs that have come from Arabic, the short vowel-markers occur twice. This indicates the presence of a short vowel as well as the consonant **n**. The commonest of these in Urdu involves the vowel symbol َ **zabar**. This indicates a short **a** and is placed over ا **alif**. The vowel, however, is not lengthened.

عادتاً	یقیناً	فوراً	مثلاً
'ādatan	**yaqīnan**	**fauran**	**masalan**
habitually	certainly	immediately	for example

The Arabic definite article ال al

The Arabic definite article ال **al** is found in certain phrases and words that have come into Urdu from Arabic, including people's names and adverbial expressions. It is not always pronounced as it appears. Often the short **a** vowel in **al** is not pronounced and, in its place, the vowel of the preceding word is pronounced. This preceding vowel is shortened if long.

بالکل	فی الحال
bi alkul	**fī alhāl**
(**bilkul**)	(**filhāl**)
absolutely	at present

When ال **al** precedes one of the following characters, ت **te**, ث **se**, د **dāl**, ذ **zāl**, ر **re**, ز **ze**, س **sīn**, ش **shīn**, ص **svād**, ض **zād**, ط **to'e**, ظ **zo'e**, ل **lām or** ن **nūn**, ل **lām** is not pronounced. In its place the character that follows is pronounced twice. Occasionally the symbol ّ **tashdīd** is written over this.

السّلام علیکم	و علیکم السّلام
assalām 'alaikum	**va'alaikum assalām**
	(**vālaikum assalām**)
a greeting	the response to this greeting
(lit: 'peace be with you')	(lit: 'and peace be with you')

Often the short vowel in ال **al** is pronounced as **u**.

دارالسلطنت	صِراج الدِین
dārussaltanat	**sirājuddīn**
capital (m)	a name (lit: 'lamp of the faith')

Further notes on pronunciation

Some words that appear in this book have a pronunciation that does not quite match the Roman transliteration. In such cases the pronunciation has been provided in parentheses. For example, a short **a** vowel followed by ہ **choṭī he** in a word-final position is often pronounced together as a long **ā** vowel. For this reason, there exist two spellings of some words in Urdu.

پتہ	or	پتا	کمرہ	or	کمرا
patah (**patā**)		**patā**	**kamrah** (**kamrā**)		**kamrā**
address (m)			room (m)		

The presence of ہ **choṭī he** or ح **baṛī he** may also influence the pronunciation of a preceding short vowel in other ways. When followed by one of these characters, short **a** and **i** vowels are occasionally pronounced as **e** in the English word **bet** and a short **u** is occasionally pronounced as **o** in the English **go**. This occurs when very little or no vowel sound follows ہ **choṭī he** or ح **baṛī he**. In the following examples, the first form given in Roman represents the transliteration while the second (in parentheses) represents the pronunciation.

پہلا	صحت	مہک	مِہربانی	مِحنت	تُحفہ
pahlā	**sahat**	**mahak**	**mihrbānī**	**mihnat**	**tuhfah**
(**pehlā**)	(**sehat**)	(**mehak**)	(**mehrbānī**)	(**mehnat**)	(**tohfā**)
first	health (f)	odour (f)	kindness (f)	labour (f)	gift (m)

However, the pronunciation of a short **a** vowel preceding either ہ **choṭī he** or ح **baṛī he** is not affected in this manner in every word where these conditions apply.

For example:

جگہ	وجہ
jagah	**vajah**
place (f)	reason (f)

The pronunciation of a few others words in which ہ **choṭī he** occurs in a final position is also irregular.

کہ	نہ	بلکہ
kah	**nah**	**balkah**
(**kĕ**)	(**na**)	(**balkĕ**)
that	no	rather

Doubling of ہ choṭī he

In some words both medial and final forms of ہ **choṭī he** occur one after the other. This is done to distinguish words in which the sound **h** is pronounced at the end from those where it occurs but is pronounced as **ā** or even **ĕ**, such as in the words پتہ **patah** (**patā**), کمرہ **kamrah** (**kamrā**) and کہ **kah** (**kĕ**), etc.

کہہ	سہہ
kahh	**sahh**
(**keh**)	(**seh**)
say	endure

Reading and writing practice

1. Read the following words and then write them in Roman script.

Meaning	Roman	Urdu
for		کے لئے (a
mirror		آئینہ (b
bicycle		سائیکل (c
may go		جائے (d
flight		فلائیٹ (e
save		بچاؤ (f

2. What sort of courses can be studied at the Islamabad Academy? Read the following advertisement and then write the Urdu in Roman script.

خواتین و حضرات	(a
بذریعہ ڈاک پڑھئے	(b
اِنگلش لینگوِج کورس	(c
اَیئر ہوسٹیس فلائیٹ اِسٹیوارڈ	(d
بیوٹی پارلر کورس	(e
اَیئر ٹِکٹنگ	(f

(g موٹر سائیکل مرمّت

(h اِسلام آباد اکیڈمی پوسٹ بکس
1237 جی پی او اسلام آباد

Glossary

ladies	خواتِین
and	و
gentlemen	حضُرات
by post	بذرِیعہ ڈاک
study (imperative)	پڑِھئے
repairing (f)	مرمّت

3. The following is an advertisement for a soft drink that is very popular in India. Transliterate the sentences into Roman script.

(b) نہ کوئی مصنوعی ذائقہ

(c) نہ کوئی کاربونیٹس

(d) نہ بناوٹی مٹھاس

(e) البتّہ قُدرتی خُوبیوں سے بھرپور

(f) ۸۵ سال سے ہم سب کا جانا پہچانا

(a) رُوح افزا شُربت

(g) ہمدرد

Glossary

sherbet (f)	شربت
no	نہ کوئی
artificial	مصنوعی
flavour (m)	ذائقہ
carbonates	کاربونیٹس
artificial	بناوٹی
sweetness (m)	مٹھاس
rather	البتّہ
natural	قدرتی
with goodness (f)	خوبیوں
for eighty-five years	۸۵ سال سے
all of our	ہم سب کا
recognised	جانا پہچانا
full of	بھرپور
name (m)	روح افزا

Summary

- The symbol ء **hamzā** is generally used to mark where one syllable in a word ends in a vowel and the next syllable begins with one.
- **izāfat** is a short **e** vowel which marks a relationship between two words. It is represented either by the vowel marker ِ **zer** or by the final form of ی **ye**, with or without ء **hamzā**. In common compounds it is occasionally omitted in the script but is pronounced. It can be translated by **of** in English.
- Several characters have modified forms, including س **sīn**, ش **shīn** and characters in the ب **be** series.
- ٰ over the character ی **ye** in a final position in some Arabic words gives the pronunciation **ā** in place of **ī**.
- The pronunciation of the Arabic definite article ال **al** depends on the characters that surround it in a word.
- ہ **choṭī he** and ح **baṛī he** often influence the pronunciation of a preceding short **a** vowel.
- Often the pronunciation of a short **a** vowel and ہ **choṭī he** at the end of a word is realised as **ā**.
- In some words in which ہ **choṭī he** is pronounced **h** at the end of a word, its medial and final forms are both written to indicate this.

Answers to practices

1. a) **ke liye** b) **āīnah** (**āīnā**) c) **sāīkal** d) **jāe** e) **flāīṭ** f) **bacāo**

2. a) **k͟havātīn ua hazrāt**, ladies and gentlemen b) **bazariya'h ḍāk** (**bazariyā**) **paṛhiye**, study by post c) **inglish laingvīj cors**, English language course d) **aiyar hosṭes flāiṭ isṭyūārḍ**, air hostess flight steward e) **byūṭī pālar cors**, beauty parlour course f) **aiyar ṭikiṭing**, air ticketing g) **moṭar sāīkal marammat**, motorcycle repairing h) **islāmābād akeḍamī posṭ baks**, **1237 jī pī o islāmābād** Islamabad Academy post box 1237 GPO Islamabad

3. a) **rūh afzā sharbat** (name of sherbet) b) **nah** (**nā**) **koī masnū'ī zāikah** (**zāikā**), no artificial flavour c) **nah** (**nā**) **koī cārboneṭs**, no carbonates d) **nah** (**nā**) **banāvaṭī miṭhās**, no artificial sweeteners (sweetness) e) **albattah** (**albattā**) **qudratī khūbiyō se bhar pūr**, rather, filled with natural goodness f) **85 sāl se ham sab kā jānā pahcānā**, for eighty-five years all of our recognised (recognised by us all) g) **hamdard**, brand name

APPENDIX

Numbers

1	**ek**	ایک	۱
2	**do**	دو	۲
3	**tīn**	تِین	۳
4	**cār**	چار	۴
5	**pā̃c**	پانچ	۵
6	**cha (chai)**	چھ	۶
7	**sāt**	سات	۷
8	**āṭh**	آٹھ	۸
9	**nau**	نو	۹
10	**das**	دس	۱۰
11	**gyārah**	گیارہ	۱۱
12	**bārah**	بارہ	۱۲

13	**terah**	تیرہ	۱۳
14	**caudah**	چَودہ	۱۴
15	**pandrah**	پَندُرہ	۱۵
16	**solah**	سولہ	۱۶
17	**satrah**	سترہ	۱۷
18	**aṭṭhārah**	اٹھّارہ	۱۸
19	**unnīs**	اُنِّیس	۱۹
20	**bīs**	بِیس	۲۰
21	**ikkīs**	اِکّیس	۲۱
22	**bāīs**	بائِیس	۲۲
23	**teīs**	تیئِیس	۲۳
24	**caubīs**	چَوبِیس	۲۴
25	**paccīs**	پچّیِس	۲۵
26	**chabbīs**	چھبّیِس	۲۶
27	**sattāīs**	ستّائِیس	۲۷
28	**aṭṭhāīs**	اٹھائیس	۲۸

29	**untīs**	اُنتِیس	۲۹
30	**tīs**	تِیس	۳۰
31	**ikattīs**	اِکتِیس	۳۱
32	**battīs**	بتِیس	۳۲
33	**taintīs**	تینَتِیس	۳۳
34	**cauntīs**	چونتِیس	۳۴
35	**paintīs**	پینَتِیس	۳۵
36	**chattīs**	چھتِّیس	۳۶
37	**saintīs**	سینَتِیس	۳۷
38	**aṛtīs**	اڑتِیس	۳۸
39	**untālīs**	اُنتالِیس	۳۹
40	**cālīs**	چالِیس	۴۰
41	**iktālīs**	اِکتالِیس	۴۱
42	**bayālīs**	بیالِیس	۴۲
43	**taintālīs**	تینتالِیس	۴۳
44	**cavālīs**	چوالِیس	۴۴

45	**paintālīs**	پَینتالِیس	۴۵
46	**chiyālīs**	چھیالِیس	۴۶
47	**saintālīs**	سینتالِیس	۴۷
48	**aṛtālīs**	اڑ تالِیس	۴۸
49	**uncās**	اُنچاس	۴۹
50	**pacās**	پچاس	۵۰
51	**ikyāvan**	اِکیاون	۵۱
52	**bāvan**	باون	۵۲
53	**tirpan**	تِرپن	۵۳
54	**cavan**	چون	۵۴
55	**pacpan**	پچپُن	۵۵
56	**chappan**	چھپّن	۵۶
57	**sattāvan**	ستّاون	۵۷
58	**aṭṭhāvan**	اٹھاون	۵۸
59	**unsaṭh**	انُسٹھ	۵۹
60	**sāṭh**	ساٹھ	۶۰

61	iksaṭh	اِکَسَٹھ	٦۱
62	bāsaṭh	باسَٹھ	٦۲
63	tresaṭh	تریسَٹھ	٦۳
64	caunsaṭh	چونسَٹھ	٦۴
65	painsaṭh	پَینسَٹھ	٦۵
66	chiyāsaṭh	چھیاسَٹھ	٦٦
67	saṛsaṭh	سَٹْرسَٹھ	٦۷
68	aṛsaṭh	اُڑسَٹھ	٦۸
69	unhattar	اُنْہَتَّر	٦۹
70	sattar	سَتَّر	۷۰
71	ikhattar	اِکْہَتَّر	۷۱
72	bahattar	بَہَتَّر	۷۲
73	tihattar	تِہَتَّر	۷۳
74	cauhattar	چَوہَتَّر	۷۴
75	pichattar	پِچْہَتَّر	۷۵
76	chihattar	چِہَتَّر	۷٦

77	**satattar**	ستتّر	۷۷
78	**aṭhattar**	اٹھتّر	۷۸
79	**unāssī**	اُناسی	۷۹
80	**assī**	اسّی	۸۰
81	**ikāsī**	اکاسی	۸۱
82	**bayāsī**	بیاسی	۸۲
83	**tirāsī**	تِراسی	۸۳
84	**caurāsī**	چَوراسی	۸۴
85	**picāsī**	پِچاسی	۸۵
86	**chiyāsī**	چھیاسی	۸۶
87	**sattāsī**	ستّاسی	۸۷
88	**aṭṭhāsī**	اٹھاسی	۸۸
89	**navāsī**	نواسی	۸۹
90	**navve**	نوّے	۹۰
91	**ikānve**	اِکانوے	۹۱
92	**bānve**	بانوے	۹۲

93	**tirānve**	تِرانوے	۹۳
94	**caurānve**	چَورانوے	۹۴
95	**picānve**	پچانوے	۹۵
96	**chiyānve**	چھیانوے	۹۶
97	**satānve**	ستانوے	۹۷
98	**aṭṭhānve**	اٹھانوے	۹۸
99	**ninānve**	نِنانوے	۹۹
100	**sau**	سَو	۱۰۰
101	**ek sau ek**	ایک سَو ایک	۱۰۱
200	**do sau**	دو سَو	۲۰۰
1,000	**ek hazār**	ایک ہزار	۱۰۰۰
10,000	**das hazār**	دس ہزار	۱۰،۰۰۰
100,000	**ek lākh**	ایک لاکھ	۱،۰۰،۰۰۰
1,000,000	**das lākh**	دس لاکھ	۱۰،۰۰،۰۰۰
10,000,000	**ek karoṛ**	ایک کروڑ	۱،۰۰،۰۰،۰۰۰
1,000,000,000	**ek arab**	ایک ارب	۱،۰۰،۰۰،۰۰،۰۰۰

Decimals and fractions

٫	اعشاریّہ
a'shāriyah	(**a'shāriyā**)
	decimal point

For example:

دو ہزار پانچ سو چوبیس اعشاریّہ دو تین

۲۵۲۴٫۲۳

do hazār pā̃c sau caubīs a'shāriyā do tīn

two thousand five hundred and twenty-four point two three

0	**sifar**	صِفر
1/4	**ek cauthāī**	ایک چَوتھائی
1/3	**ek tihāī**	ایک تِہائی
1/2	**ādhā**	آدھا
2/3	**do tihāī**	دو تِہائی
3/4	**paun** or **tīn cauthāī**	پَون تین چَوتھائی
1 1/4	**savā**	سوا

1 1/2	**ḍeṛh**	ڈیڑھ
1 3/4	**paune do**	پَونے دو
2 1/4	**savā do**	سوا دو
2 1/2	**ḍhāī**	ڈھائی
3 1/2	**sāṛhe tīn**	ساڑھے تِین

From 3 1/2 onwards the word ساڑھے **sāṛhe** precedes the numeral to add one-half.

For example:

ساڑھے چار

sāṛhe cār
4 1/2

Dates

Dates are indicated by placing the word ؁ **sanh** (year) without the dot under the numerals together with an abbreviation of the word عیسوی **'īsvī** (Christian era).

For example:

؁۱۹۴۷ء

1947

Days of the week

پیر **pīr** Monday	منگل **mangal** Tuesday	بدھ **budh** Wednesday	جمعرات **jum'a rāt (jumerāt)** Thursday
جمعہ **jum'a (jumā)** Friday	ہفتہ سنیچر **haftah (haftā)/ sanīcar** Saturday	اتوار **itvār** Sunday	

Months

Christian calendar

جنوری **janvarī** January	فروری **farvarī** February	مارچ **mārc** March	اپریل **aprail** April
مئی **maī** May	جون **jūn** June	جولائی **jūlāī** July	اگست **agast** August
ستمبر **sitambar** September	اکتوبر **aktūbar** October	نومبر **navambar** November	دسمبر **disambar** December

Muslim calendar

The Muslim calendar dates from July 16, 622 AD. This is the day after the departure of the prophet Muhammad from Medina to Mecca. Dates according to this calendar are followed by the word ہجری **hijrī** from the word ہجرہ **hijrah** (**hijrā**) which means 'flight'. This is abbreviated with the symbol ھ .

محرّم **muharram**	صفر **safar**	ربیع الاوّل **rabī'ul avval**	ربیع الثانی **rabī'us sānī**
جمادی الاوّل **jumādī ul avval**	جمادی الثانی **jumādī us sānī**	رجب **rajab**	شعبان **sha'bān (shābān)**
رمضان **ramzān**	شوال **shavvāl**	ذی قعدہ **zī qa'dah (zīqād)**	ذی الحجّہ **zī ul hijjah (zulhij)**

Other related titles

TEACH YOURSELF

URDU

David Matthews and Mohamed Kasim Dalvi

This is a complete course in spoken and written Urdu. If you have never learnt Urdu before, or if your Urdu needs brushing up, *Teach Yourself Urdu* is for you.

The authors have created a practical course that is both fun and easy to work through. They explain everything along the way and give you plenty of opportunities to practise what you have learnt. The course structure means that you can work at your own pace, arranging your learning to suit your needs.

The course contains:

- A range of graded units of dialogues, culture notes, grammar and exercises
- A step-by-step guide to pronunciation
- An Urdu–English vocabulary

By the end of the course you'll be able to cope with a whole range of situations and use the language confidently.